SIR HALLEY STEWART TRUST: PUBLICATIONS

Volume 10

SIR HALLEY STEWART

SIR HALLEY STEWART

Preacher, Politician,
Businessman, Benefactor:
Founder of The Sir Halley
Stewart Trust

DAVID NEWTON

Foreword by
SIR STANLEY UNWIN

LONDON AND NEW YORK

First published in 1968 by George Allen & Unwin Ltd.

This edition first published in 2025
by Routledge
4 Park Square, Milton Park, Abingdon, Oxon OX14 4RN

and by Routledge
605 Third Avenue, New York, NY 10158

Routledge is an imprint of the Taylor & Francis Group, an informa business

© 1968 George Allen & Unwin Ltd.

All rights reserved. No part of this book may be reprinted or reproduced or utilised in any form or by any electronic, mechanical, or other means, now known or hereafter invented, including photocopying and recording, or in any information storage or retrieval system, without permission in writing from the publishers.

Trademark notice: Product or corporate names may be trademarks or registered trademarks, and are used only for identification and explanation without intent to infringe.

British Library Cataloguing in Publication Data
A catalogue record for this book is available from the British Library

ISBN: 978-1-032-88962-7 (Set)
ISBN: 978-1-032-88643-5 (Volume 10) (hbk)
ISBN: 978-1-032-88648-0 (Volume 10) (pbk)
ISBN: 978-1-003-53887-5 (Volume 10) (ebk)

DOI: 10.4324/9781003538875

Publisher's Note
The publisher has gone to great lengths to ensure the quality of this reprint but points out that some imperfections in the original copies may be apparent.

Disclaimer
The publisher has made every effort to trace copyright holders and would welcome correspondence from those they have been unable to trace.

This book is a re-issue originally published in 1968. The language used and views portrayed are a reflection of its era and no offence is meant by the Publishers to any reader by this re-publication.

Sir Halley Stewart at 92
Portrait by John Frye Bourne at present in the possession of Sir Halley's grand-daughter, Dr Joan Haram

Companion volume:

The Life of Alexander Stewart,
Prisoner of Napoleon and Preacher of the Gospel

Based on his personal diary

George Allen & Unwin, Ltd. 1948

SIR HALLEY STEWART

PREACHER   POLITICIAN   BUSINESSMAN   BENEFACTOR

Founder of the
SIR HALLEY STEWART TRUST

BY

DAVID NEWTON

Foreword by
SIR STANLEY UNWIN
K.C.M.G., Hon.LL.D.(Aberdeen)

Published for
THE SIR HALLEY STEWART TRUST
by GEORGE ALLEN & UNWIN, LTD
40 MUSEUM STREET, LONDON, W.C.1

FIRST PUBLISHED IN 1968

This book is copyright under the Berne Convention. Apart from any fair dealing for the purpose of private study, research, criticism or review, as permitted under the Copyright Act, 1956, no portion may be reproduced by any process without written permission. Enquiries should be addressed to the publishers.

© *George Allen & Unwin Ltd* 1968

SBN 04 922023 3

PRINTED IN GREAT BRITAIN
in 12 on 13pt *Garamond type*
BY UNWIN BROS. LIMITED
WOKING AND LONDON

SIR HALLEY STEWART: CHRONOLOGY

Born Chipping Barnet	January 18, 1838
Clerk, Robert Davis & Co., Shoreditch bankers	1853
Clerk, Hill, Wood & Hughes, Coal factors	1856
Clerk, Smith & Co., brewers, Hastings	1862
Started Sunday School, Croft Chapel, Hastings	April 1863
Minister, Croft Chapel	September 1863
Marriage	June 20, 1865
Oil cake mill started, Branbridges	1870
Moved to Beaufort House, St Leonards	1872
Minister, Caledonian Road Chapel, Islington	1873
Left ministry for politics	1877
Founded *Hastings and St Leonards Times*	1877
Moved to Park Mansion, St Leonards	1879
Rochester mills erected	1879–80
Election agent for East Sussex Liberal candidates	1880
Sold Hastings newspaper	1883
Rochester mills destroyed by fire	November 15, 1884
First defeat in Spalding election (by Finch-Hatton)	December 2, 1885
Second defeat at Spalding (by Finch-Hatton)	July 10, 1886

First victory at Spalding (beat Tryon)	July 1, 1887
Second victory at Spalding (beat Pollock)	November 15, 1892
Allotments and Smallholdings Association formed, Halley Stewart president	1893
Moved to The Firs, Clapham Park	1894
Third defeat at Spalding (by Pollock)	1895
Rochester mills sold to B.O.C.M. Ltd	1899
Defeated in Peterborough election (by Purvis)	October 5, 1900
B. J. Forder & Co. Ltd (bricks) formed	1900
Moved to 'Wardown', Luton	1900
Moved to The Red House, Harpenden	1904
Victory in Greenock election (beat Reid)	January 18, 1906
Guest at Royal Garden Party	1908
Retired from Parliament on dissolution	January 1910
In Asquith's list of potential peers	1911
Forder lime and cement works sold to British Portland Cement Manufacturers Ltd	1912
Golden wedding	June 20, 1915
Resigned chair of London Brick Company Ltd	1924
Founded Harpenden Liberal Association	1924

Founded Trust	December 15, 1924
Death of Mrs Stewart	December 26, 1924
Ninetieth birthday lunch for Smallholders Association	1928
Opened Stewartby Memorial Hall	1930
Knighthood in New Year Honours	1932
In party to welcome Duke of Kent to Stewartby	1935
Ninety-ninth birthday	January 18, 1937
Death at Harpenden	January 26, 1937

FOREWORD

By Sir Stanley Unwin
K.C.M.G., Hon. LL.D (Aberdeen)
Chairman, The Sir Halley Stewart Trust

Few now remain who knew Sir Halley Stewart in the flesh. As teacher, preacher, speaker, political worker, Member of Parliament, businessman, philanthropist and committed Christian, he was both in outlook and activity an outstanding figure throughout his long years of service.

To a privileged group of us he entrusted the great honour and challenge of seeking to bring to current problems the principles, the passion and the conviction which made him so great a champion in his own day of those in need.

He endowed the Sir Halley Stewart Trust not only with funds to ensure a continuance of his lifelong work of faith in God and care for God's creatures, but also with memories of a splendid personal example of belief and love in action. One of the most remarkable things about Sir Halley was that even in his nineties he was, in ideas and outlook, one of the youngest of the Trustees.

We who knew him can never forget him—but generations are around us who knew him not. For their sake, for the sake of those who will administer the Trust after us, and of those who will be its grantees, we are glad to make this brief record of Sir Halley Stewart's life available. Our hope is that those who read it will discover for themselves something of that Stewart fire which has so wonderfully warmed us in our own day. *January 1968*

ACKNOWLEDGMENTS

THE Trustees of the Sir Halley Stewart Trust acknowledge with deep gratitude their debt to those who assembled, prepared and presented the material for this biography.

Mrs D. Gunnell devoted some years to delving deeply into scattered published and unpublished records to provide a substantial preliminary manuscript. We are indeed grateful to her for her lengthy and painstaking work, and for producing a detailed script which is treasured among the Trust's archives, and of which the British Museum has accepted a copy.

The present printed text is by David Newton. He not only drew extensively upon the original work of Mrs Gunnell but also upon further private papers, a host of personal memories, and additional records in many places.

The Trustees wish to record their sincere gratitude to David Newton for recreating the character of the Trust's revered founder as it is presented in this volume.

CONTENTS

	SIR HALLEY STEWART: A CHRONOLOGY	7
	FOREWORD	11
	ACKNOWLEDGMENTS	13
1.	FATHER AND FAMILY	19
2.	MINISTRY, MARRIAGE AND MILLING	31
3.	PULPIT TO POLITICS	42
4.	INTO PARLIAMENT	51
5.	THE BUSY MEMBER	63
6.	LAND FOR THE LABOURER	75
7.	OUT OF MILLING	83
8.	INTO BRICKS: IN AT GREENOCK	90
9.	POTENTIAL PEER	102
10.	IN TRUST	113
11.	A HOUSE MOURNS ITS MISTRESS	121
12.	HALLEY AT HOME	132
13.	THE TRUST AT WORK	142
14.	KNIGHT BACHELOR	154
15.	THE HUNDREDTH YEAR	170
	APPENDICES: Titles of Trust Lectures	180
	Names of Trustees	182
	Stewart Family Trees	183
	INDEX	189

ILLUSTRATIONS

Portrait at ninety-two	*frontispiece*
The Young Preacher Halley's brother Ebenezer	*facing page* 64
Jane and Halley Stewart	65
Reception at The Red House for Trust Research Fellows	80
Sir Halley's coat of arms Alexander's seal	81
Facsimile letter to Stanley Unwin	*page* 144

1. FATHER AND FAMILY

AT the Connaught Rooms, London, on Monday, March 15, 1937, a group of influential businessmen stood in silence in memory of Sir Halley Stewart. It was the day of the annual general meeting of the London Brick Company Limited, and they had just heard a tribute paid to this remarkable man by his remarkable son, Sir P. Malcolm Stewart, speaking as chairman and one of the managing directors of the company.

Sir Halley, who had died in his hundredth year seven weeks earlier at The Red House, his Harpenden home, was senior deputy chairman of the London Brick Company, having stood down as chairman in favour of Sir Malcolm in 1924. 'He was the principal founder of the business we are carrying on today,' said Sir Malcolm in his tribute. 'It owes much to his good judgment and to his sound financial instincts, based on a practical knowledge of accountancy—which I gratefully acknowledge he imparted to me in my youth.'

How right it was that the figures, statistics and resolutions making up the business of this winter day in 1937 should yield place at the outset to a son's vivid memories of the outstanding features of Sir Halley Stewart's life and character. Everyone in that room that morning, and thousands beyond its walls, were in debt to him. Thousands more today and tomorrow find—and will find him still—their benefactor through the enterprises he built up, the principles he proclaimed, the example he set, the Trust he founded, and the continuing research made possible by it.

His life spanned a century. Office clerk, teacher, and preacher, Halley Stewart went on to make his name known in business, in journalism and in politics. He made two fortunes, declared that he would never die 'disgracefully rich', and left most of his wealth to the Trust he founded for research 'towards the Christian ideal in all social life'. He was born in 1838, the year after Queen Victoria came to the throne, and died in his hundredth year, before the Second World War could ring down the final curtain on the strange inter-war period into which he had survived.

A man endowed with great vitality and intellect, Halley Stewart's burning convictions, his indomitable independence and his passion for justice left their mark on everything he touched. In him it seemed that the fine qualities of many forebears were fused together to make one rich, strong, whole man. But to find the source of his worth the hardy Stewart stream need not be traced far back, for few men had such a father as Halley. Here was a man indeed, a man whose story has already been told, and that largely in his own words as penned for his family circle.

'I have no property to leave you,' wrote the Rev. Alexander Stewart sometime in the 1840's, 'yet I have something to leave you—a few reminiscences of my past life, which has been characterized by chequered peculiarities.' He wished his narrative (always referred to by his family as 'the diary') to warn and to stimulate his children and 'to impress deeply on their minds the doctrine of Divine Providence, and the great fact that special divine influences can and do effect marvellous changes on the thoughts, sentiments, and conduct of men'. Tied in red tape, the handwritten manuscript for years lay in Sir Halley's private safe till, when past ninety, he gave it to Sir Malcolm and the publication of an edited version became possible.[1]

Alexander was born in 1790 in Kirkcaldy, Fifeshire, third of a family of twelve. His father's family had farmed for generations on the north side of the Grampians, where there had been early settlements of Highland Stewarts in both the Atholl and the Mar country. His mother's maiden name was Halley. Her maternal forebears had the farm of Orphet in Strathmeglie for almost 550 years. There were deaths and anxieties in the Kirkcaldy family but it was a happy family and an affectionate one. It was only the evil persuasion of a young and unkind companion which led Alexander at fourteen to run away to sea in 1804. On board he found nothing but toil, discomfort, oaths and unkindness as the ships he served on plied their coastal trade. Twice he escaped drowning after falling overboard; once he was shipwrecked, and once, when tacking the ship, the block of the main sheet swung against his head and almost killed him.

In January 1805, nine months before Trafalgar, the ship was captured off Brighton by a French privateer, and so began the ten years of incredible sufferings as a French prisoner of war sustained—and vividly described—by Alexander. Long marches, hunger, cold, boredom, temptation, the grim rigours of one French fortress after another, tested and stretched the young Scot in body, mind and spirit during his most impressionable years. A friendship here, a hard-earned privilege there, the occasional chance to earn by prison toil, relieved the pressure from time to time.

[1] *The Life of Alexander Stewart, Prisoner of Napoleon and Preacher of the Gospel.* Written by himself to 1815, abridged by Dr Albert Peel to 1874, with a preface by his grandson, Sir P. Malcolm Stewart, Bt. London: George Allen & Unwin Ltd., 1948.

For the rest, 'all was low, all was vulgar, all was debasing'.

When Alexander could learn anything from other prisoners he seized the chance, and also profited from the meagre educational facilities which a grudging French Government permitted. Writing, arithmetic, navigation, English grammar, French language—he hungrily absorbed all that came his way. Not only this, but 'here I very naturally sucked in the first elements of that perfect hatred of tyranny which I have felt through life, and on the other hand, that deep feeling which sympathizes but little with aristocratic gradations in society, while it can fully respect talents, morals, and experience'.

In February 1811 Alexander escaped from Sarrelibre, Alsace, with three companions by sliding down a rope. This cut through his hand to expose all the bones—an injury which marked him for life. Recaptured after a week, he was marched off, chained to the others, to Verdun, his shoes disintegrating on the way and exposing his feet to the torture of icy and stony roads. After a time in the fortress of Bitche, Alexander and ninety-nine others in 1813 marched 800 miles to Briançon in the Alps. The treatment experienced there was unforgettably barbarous, but Alexander, though only a stripling, proved himself in a new way by tackling the bully of the prisoners' quarters, a big man and a boxer but not a match for the youngster's courage and burning indignation.

Various moves brought Alexander into Normandy in 1814, from where it was not difficult to reach St Malo and get aboard an English sloop of war waiting to pick up any who could escape. English indifference to their plight puzzled and hurt Alexander as he and his companions tramped from Portsmouth to London.

In so sorry a state, he refused to find refuge in the Kirkcaldy home. True, he wrote to his mother to tell of his return, but pride kept him hanging about the docks till he could join a ship and earn financial independence—and a new wardrobe—before presenting himself to his family.

See him then in May 1814 sailing for Russia, and talking of religion to the pious ship's carpenter who lent him Young's *Night Thoughts* and other Christian books. From Young he learned these lines: 'With joy, with grief, the healing hand I see, The skies it formed, and yet it bled for me'. The lines then learned never left his memory, and his sons heard him quote them with emotion on his death bed in 1874.

Alexander's troubles were not over. Back from Russia, coastal trade took the ship to Shields, where he went ashore and suffered the humiliation and bitterness of being press-ganged. However, his own captain, 'secretly moved by that Being whose ways are so mysterious', obtained his release, and with him he sailed back to London. Now at last, in January 1815, could he be paid off and make his way home to a moving reunion with his now widowed mother and his surviving brothers and sisters.

It was his knowledge of French which led Alexander to start teaching in Kirkcaldy, soon adding navigation and general subjects, and prescribing for himself a rigorous course of self-education. Taking posts in scholastic establishments was a natural progress, though soon it took him away from home to schools in and near London. The daily papers gave him a new interest in politics, and Peterloo, the Chartist massacre in Manchester, highlighted its radical turn. Voltaire and other French and English infidels had affected his religious thinking but now an uneasy conscience drove him to study Christian evidences, and unforgotten effects of schoolday bigotry led him into Dissent.

As an assistant to James Lemon, at his school in Holloway, he began to lead school worship, formed a local church, and when friends suggested training for the ministry, became a student at Hoxton College, which served the Independent churches. At a playground presentation at the end of term, Mr Lemon could not speak highly enough of his assistant. 'Mr Stewart is a remarkable man,' he said. 'Whatever he does, he does it with all his heart. . . .'

It was by teaching at Lemon's school two afternoons a week that Alexander not only paid his way through college but continued to pay his mother's rent. Many things were against him as he strove to fit himself for ministerial life. He had a half-Scottish and half-foreign accent, and sea-faring associations coloured his speech. His hardships were no preparation for the corporate life of a college, and his hard-gained store of knowledge was far from the ordered academic study on which his comrades could look back.

Despite hardships which would have crushed a lesser man, he retained great physical strength and had a commanding figure, combined with self-discipline, a great capacity for work and an unusual gift for leadership and decision. He had courage, he had determination, he had personality, and he attracted the affection and regard which such qualities never fail to evoke. To step down to the position of an ordinary student and place himself under academic discipline was a test of the depth of his conviction that he was truly called to the ministry. Alexander was up at five each morning, eager to pack into the day all that he could. He learned how to discuss and converse, being for most of his time in college the president of its debating society, and it was not long before he was acknowledged as the leader of the student body. In 1823 he became minister of the Congregational church in Wood Street, Chipping Barnet, but not before declining a series of other invitations: to the church at Manningtree, to a missionary college in Malacca, to a tutorship in Moscow, and to the Superintendency of the Madagascar Mission—a list which is testimony itself to the impression he had made in church circles. Halley Stewart was one of fourteen children born in the manse at Barnet. Such was his father, a man whose character and accomplishments were both the springboard and the background of Halley's own remarkable life. Inevitably the son reflects the father, and the father's life and person are enlightening as a commentary upon the son's career.[1]

And what of Halley's mother? Ann Kezia White was a child of the Barnet church. Alexander preached there for some months before leaving college in May 1823. Within a year, on January 13, 1824, when he was thirty-three, he was married to one of seven daughters who helped fill a family pew near the pulpit. She was twenty-four, and they started life together in the chapel house on £100 a year. One of the oldest letters extant in the Stewart family, dated

[1] The BBC drew on the published Life of Alexander for material for a schools radio programme broadcast on June 5, 1958, in the series on exemplary characters entitled 'Stories from British History'. It was a dramatized reconstruction of his noteworthy career, those taking part being Doris Nichols, Peter Ducrow and Harold Reese of the Schools Repertory Company, and Alaric Cotter, Nigel Anthony and Cavan Malone, free-lance actors.

January 19, 1824, was written just after the wedding by the bride's mother to Mrs Rose Hawkes of Royston, an old family friend. Mrs White describes moving with her family to a house in a healthier spot farther from Town and goes on:

'This circumstance has however led to a result I did not in the least anticipate at the time, namely, the union in bonds of matrimony of Ann my eldest Daughter with the Revd. Alexander Stewart, minister of the independent church and congregation at Barnet —the ceremony was perform'd last Tuesday morning at Covent Garden church (without any bustle), none but our own immediate friends being present, and the young folks have since that day been in Lodgings at Hammersmith four miles from Town—scarcely however has a day passed without their visiting Brydges Street and on Friday last they came in while Mr E. K. Fordham was with me in the dining room— it is their present purpose to return to Barnet on Thursday next.

'You will I am persuaded be desirous of knowing something of Ann's partner, at least what are my thoughts respecting him, and it is my wish to gratify you well knowing the interest you feel in what concerns me and mine. He is a young Scotchman from Fife, of suitable age (a little older than Ann) and of agreeable person and manners, very intelligent and of good classical education—I trust also that altho' rather of an argumentative turn of mind, yet most decidedly pious, and most sincerely devoted to the cause and interest of the dear Redeemer. A very considerable revival has taken place at Barnet since his residence there, and we sincerely hope his gracious Master has yet much for him to do in that place. An enlargement of the chapel, or the pulling it down and erecting another is in agitation, but I rather think it will be the former on account of the expence.

'I have thus given you my respected friend a general outline of the circumstances, and on the part of my dear child have only to request your acceptace of the accompanying piece of bridal cake in token of her affectionate regards, as well as those of

Your sincere Friend, P. WHITE."

As it happened, by October 1824, under Alexander's leadership, a new church and a new house replaced the somewhat dilapidated buildings. By 1827 he was taking in boarders and dayboys to increase his income by teaching, and a year later added a schoolroom. In addition, in 1833 he began to admit students to coach them for the Nonconformist training colleges. Understandably, there were tempting offers to serve in other challenging posts at home or overseas, and recognition of Alexander's work twice included him in deputations to Queen Victoria. On July 17, 1837, he was in a deputation presenting an address on behalf of the Dissenting denominations on the Queen's accession, and was similarly included in a party to the palace on her coronation.

The increasing needs of his large family led Alexander in 1847 to take over Lemon's school, where he had once taught, at Palmer House, Holloway, though he continued to preach at Barnet till 1850. The Barnet school was carried on, but only for a time, for Palmer House prospered and also gave employment to his sons Alexander, Philip and John. In time their father moved out to Camden Road, but kept in touch with family and school affairs even though he relinquished control of the school in 1864, when he was seventy-four. Throughout life his income never exceeded £250 per annum.

Of the fourteen children born to Alexander and Ann in the house next to the Barnet church, Halley was the tenth, and the fifth son, his birthday being January 18, 1838. His father had by then been in Barnet for fifteen years, and what with church and local affairs, the scholars and the students—to say nothing of the minister's own large family—the manse and the church buildings were in a continual fever of activity. Alexander dominated it all. What a picture Halley would have of him! Family prayers, public preaching, school lecturing, platform persuasion, mealtime argument, domestic fun, wrestling with students, sharing private griefs, restraining drunken bullies—a man of belief and prayer, a man of energy and action, a real man indeed. The faith which had kept Alexander clean and strong through the perils of imprisonment, the hazards of seafaring, and the burdens of church and school, was for Halley incarnate in his father. For Halley himself it became similarly deeply real and personal. Indeed, we shall see as we go on to trace Halley's life and character that Mrs White's personal assessment of Alexander, made in her letter to Mrs Hawkes in 1824, can in part be applied aptly enough to Alexander's son.

There were plenty of opportunities for religion to be seen in practical ways, ways in which the Stewart children were called to lend a hand. There were always guests and visitors to make comfortable and innumerable chores connected with church and school. There were parties and meetings, errands to the homes of members of the congregation, and all the inescapable tasks that made daily demands on hand and foot and temper. Each day had its routine.

Handwritten recollections of Barnet by Philip, the second son, give this as a typical Sunday programme, starting with a prayer meeting at 7 a.m. for the students and others: 8.0 breakfast, 9.0 school Scripture class, 9.30 Sunday School, 11.0 church service, 1.0 dinner, 2.30 Sunday School followed by a walk, 5.0 tea, 6.30 church service, 8.0 singing in the home, where the flute, violin, clarinet and bass viol (as used at the services) would again be heard.

Chipping Barnet, on the Great North Road out of London, was at this time still alive with coaching traffic. The highway passed across the end of Wood Street a mere 200 yards from the manse, and running alongside the coaches as they passed through the town was one of the delights of the frolicsome Stewart boys. Philip described the domestic life of the family in intimate detail and Barnet scenes as Halley must have known them are faithfully pictured. He saw the 'Peelers' keeping order at Barnet Fair in their top hats, tail coats and white trousers; the country women and tradesfolk crying their wares along the streets; the early railway carriages, hard-seated and open to the weather; the austere gentlemen who came to chapel in their carriages, and the homely women and the manual workers with their gnarled hands. He was four when Parliament banned the employment of small boys by chimney sweeps.

It was the time of the Hungry Forties and of a wave of emigration; the Chartist movement had achieved some of its aims in the First Reform Act of 1832; slavery had just been abolished in the British Empire (Alexander knew Wilberforce); Catholics had been allowed to enter Parliament; and the first co-operative store was soon to open in Rochdale. In 1847 when Halley was nine, Carlyle, Ruskin, Tennyson, John

Stuart Mill, Dickens, Livingstone and Lord Shaftesbury were among the great of the day. Wellington was an old man; Disraeli and Gladstone were settling into their Parliamentary careers; Abraham Lincoln's presidency was still twelve years away. The young Queen was bringing a new dignity to the Throne.

This was the year, too, when Halley first showed his genius for handling money. Rather than spend the penny given to him to pay the toll at Highgate, he would make a long detour and so save the coin! The year 1847 also saw Alexander moving from Chipping Barnet to take over the Palmer House School at Holloway—a palatial place compared with the manse and, at the time it was built, the last house between Holloway and Highgate. The main part of this substantial building had a stately bow front. Three-storey wings flanked it on both sides. Here Halley completed his education. He was a natural leader and his father preferred to send him rather than his less dominating brothers whenever there was a squabble to settle among the pupils. For himself, he found school discipline irksome, and Alexander wisely allowed him small responsibilities which tended to alter his attitude and to hint at the man who would always find it easier to control than to obey.

2. MINISTRY, MARRIAGE AND MILLING

Halley would have been glad to continue his studies and follow his father as a schoolmaster, but Philip, whose venture in setting up a school of his own at Braintree had failed, and George, whose ill-health had cut short his training for the ministry, both returned to Palmer House. So in 1853 Halley was sent into the world to earn his own living. He began as a clerk in Shoreditch at £30 a year, in the private banking house of Robert Davis and Co. It was a great education in the worth of money, and later he was to tell his sons that it was to their disadvantage that they were so well off when they started. One of these sons, Percy Malcolm, mentioned his father's early days in the City when speaking of him at the London Brick Company annual meeting soon after his death. 'I remember his telling me that he could get a luncheon of a dozen good oysters, bread and butter, and half-a-pint of stout for sevenpence,' he recalled.

In March 1854 the Crimean War overshadowed the business world, but days in the bank were uneventful until Halley fell in love with the daughter of one of its wealthy clients. When her father took steps to end the association between his genteel child and the ten-hour-a-day clerk, the shock opened his eyes wide to the rigid class distinction of the time. The upset, however, did not blind him to business prospects, and Halley became increasingly critical of what he called 'the reckless method with which the bank's business was pursued'. Though offered double his salary to remain, he left the bank and it is a remarkable tribute to his understanding of the situation, though only nineteen, that shortly afterwards it had to suspend payment.

Halley's second position was with Messrs Hill, Wood and Hughes, coal factors. In 1857, soon after changing jobs, he paid his first visit to the House of Commons and heard a speech by Palmerston as Prime Minister and an attack on him by Gladstone. He was so enthralled by the scene and so captivated by Gladsone's powers as a speaker that an attendant had to warn him to sit still. His sympathies were with the under-privileged, with the workers and with the poor. There was plenty to occupy his mind in the clamant call for social justice. Nor was he an armchair devotee of an airy idealism. Home had taught him the value of education. Compulsory education for all was years away but ragged schools had made their appearance in London, and Halley, with an old school friend named Edward Spicer, gave many leisure hours to teaching in such a school in Bethnal Green.

Meanwhile family links were being established at Hastings. His sister Kezia, six years his senior, had opened a seminary for young ladies at Saxon House, 1 Trinity Street, her partner being an old school friend, Jane Elizabeth Atkinson, daughter of Mr Joseph Atkinson of Upper Norwood. Halley decided to leave the coal factors and in (probably) 1862 took lodgings in the same street and obtained work at the Court House Brewery of Smith and Co. George, the third brother, had been minister at the Croft Chapel in Hastings but it had been closed for a year following George's departure for Newcastle. As an office clerk in new surroundings, Halley must have had many heart-searchings and prayers as to the future and to his possible usefulness to his generation. They issued, after due consultation with Alexander and with Henry Allon, an old student of his father and a confidant since childhood, in Halley deciding to enter the ministry.

April 1863 sees him settled at 2 Croft Place, with fifty books from his father's library in his lodgings and the empty Croft Chapel building next door. His first task is to start a Sunday School, and within a month he has eighty children in the town's first Congregational Sunday School. By September the chapel is re-opened and Halley invited, at twenty-five, to become its pastor, though he was never ordained. In October a clock and bookcase were presented to him as a thank-offering for his zealous care in the formation of the church. New glory had come to the old wooden building which, built in 1803, had the distinction of being the first Nonconformist place of worship in Hastings.

The great impression Halley made as a preacher and leader was not confined to his own flock. He joined issue with unfriendly clerics and preached in other churches to encourage Nonconformist ministers and congregations. Nature endowed him with gifts that supported his powerful faith and intellect. He had a strong and handsome face, a persuasive tongue which lost little through a slight huskiness, and great clarity of expression. He spoke with conviction and sureness, and to those who considered he was perhaps too self-reliant he did not feel it wrong to say 'It's not my fault if I can see further through a brick wall than most people.' To Alexander, who often preached at Croft and guided the young minister through his early years as a pastor, Halley explained that 'every man who has ever done anything worthwhile feels some consciousness of his powers of success'.

He was a true Independent. Religion was essentially personal—a matter between a man and God alone. He distrusted Rome, for no priest should ever interpose himself between a man and his conscience. Civil liberty was essential if the cause of the people was to prevail, but he put religious liberty first because it was largely on this that civil liberty depended. Halley's view of the Bible was that it was the antidote against errors of all kinds, a book of Divine principles which should be allowed to test all action and every thought.

Often a minister, a bachelor minister, and especially a minister who, unafraid, must speak out all that is in him, is a lonely figure. In Halley's case the edge was taken off his loneliness by the presence in Hastings of Kezia and Jane. Prospering, they moved their school to the larger Norman House in Claremont, and Halley's help with the accounts of the growing establishment was welcome. Halley had been an admirer of Jane ever since her early visits to Palmer House and her companionship, understanding and sympathy both delighted and helped him now that he had the cares of a church. They were married on June 20, 1865, his father officiating at the service in the Holloway Congregational church, Camden Road, near the Stewart home.

Sadly but perhaps not unexpectedly, sister Kezia found it difficult to adjust to the new situation, and it was arranged that Halley, with the help of Jane's own means, should buy Kezia's share of the business. Then he engaged extra teaching staff and proceeded steadily to build up the school in size and prestige. A school and a church would have kept most men busy, but Halley had energy and capacity, and made time to pursue many other activities connected with religion. His work with the ragged school movement gave him a keen and active interest in education; he spoke on behalf of the missionary societies; he helped form a Hastings branch of the Lord's Day Observance Society; and when the 1867 Reform Act extended the franchise to town workers he lectured on the need to educate the new voters. At a time when only half the country's children went to school he advocated the establishment of non-sectarian schools where, however, religious instruction would be given.

Into these interests he brought his church and congregation, for his sermons—pouring from his pulpit and brought home to them by persuasive voice, eager gesture, apt anecdote, utter sincerity and obstinate conviction—allowed no division between sacred and secular, between politics and religion. He left no-one in any doubt as to what characteristics should mark a Christian nation. It was inevitable that the Liberal Party's fight for Parliamentary reform and for social progress should find him in the forefront in his adopted town. Advised by his critics to confine himself to his work as a minister, Halley told a meeting that 'every Christian man should be a Christian citizen'. His forthrightness hurt. It showed itself at one political meeting when a man in the audience got his own back by throwing a cabbage at Halley, for which he was in due course fined ten shillings with costs.

Lord Palmerston died in 1865 while in office as Prime Minister and Lord Russell succeeded him, but by 1866 Gladstone, in his prime at fifty-seven, was virtually leader of the party. In the 1868 General Election, Gladstone led the party to victory and settled down to initiate long overdue reforms during his first administration. It was the emergence of Gladstone that finally set ablaze the political fire that had already begun to burn with slow sureness in the heart and mind of Halley Stewart. He said of Gladstone: 'It was in 1866 that he took the reins to lead the people of this great Empire forward in the path of progress. Then began my Liberalism in earnest. . . .'

It was the year, too, that saw family joys and sorrows multiply. Ernest Halley, the first child born to Halley and Jane, survived only six months after his birth in July 1866. A year later, Herbert Fowler was born, again to live only six months. In October 1868, twin boys, Edgar Halley and Reginald Halley, came to fill the gap but Edgar was lost to them after a fortnight. Bertie Jane Louise, the only daughter, was born in January 1871, joined in May 1872 by another brother, Percy Malcolm. Twin sons, Eustace Halley and Bernard Halley, were born in May 1874, but history repeated itself and after only six weeks, Eustace was lost to the family following vaccination.

Old Alexander Stewart baptized some of his grandchildren and on each occasion presented them with a sovereign, though Halley refused to let him do this when Reginald was baptized in 1868. One of the last of these baptisms was of Percy Malcolm, on September 14, 1872, when Alexander and Ann were living in retirement at Branbridges, Kent. Here on November 3, 1874 Alexander died in his eighty-fifth year. Eight sons stood at the graveside when the funeral was conducted by two of the many men he had helped train for the ministry. One of them was Dr Henry Allon, who twice became chairman of the Congregational Union of England and Wales and remained one of Halley's closest friends up to his death in 1892. Ann lived on for just six more months. The two had shared an overflowing life of service together and had survived into calmer years long enough to celebrate their golden wedding, which was the occasion of a family gathering at Branbridges on January 13, 1874, and of a poem composed by their third son, George Stewart.[1]

But none of these private sorrows dimmed Halley's ardour for public progress. He agitated in Hastings against the price of gas, welcomed the introduction of electricity, advocated the opening of a free library, gave evidence at the House of Lords in favour of improved railway facilities for the resort, and frequently wrote pungent letters to the local newspaper (one of these protested against the furious and improper driving of horse-drawn trade vehicles at a speed of ten miles per hour). Meanwhile his ministry continued, he was in great demand as a speaker in chapels over a wide radius, the school was developing, and his family was growing. Halley had quickly established himself in Hastings as a noteworthy figure. A photograph taken about this time, in preaching gown, shows that a beard has thickened over his strong face, and that his countenance perfectly expresses the determined spirit within. His beloved Jane has a face more firm than beautiful, but sympathy and calm can be seen there, and enchanting ringlets reach down almost to the shoulders.

Family needs, restless energy and still untapped capacity would seem to make further venturings inevitable for Halley, but it was not until 1869 that he found himself nominally in business—apart from his

[1] References in the poem to Alexander's seal and motto are quoted in Chapter 14 in connection with Sir Halley Stewart's grant of arms.

school interest. For this he had to thank brother Ebenezer, his senior by three years, who was still a bachelor living with his parents in London. After experience with City merchants, Ebenezer had five years as a partner with Joseph Starkey & Co., Regent Street, gold and silver lacemen and embroiderers; learned underwriting at Lloyds; then joined A. F. Dickeson, whom he first met on the cricket field, as Dickeson and Stewart, commission merchants in Leadenhall Street.

Ebenezer had a great regard for Halley. They shared a serious outlook upon life and were united in a sense of responsibility toward their day and generation. They saw in Liberalism and in the Congregational churches two closely linked avenues along which they could press their personal support of the reforming and uplifting movements of the time. Halley as preacher and politician, Ebenezer as enlightened businessman strengthening the material foundation of the joint enterprise—this was the ideal which brought them together in business and which was to run like a golden thread through all the years of the partnership which followed. This, too, was the spur behind the commercial success they were to achieve.

In 1869, then, Ebenezer put his plans into operation by inviting Halley to join him as a sleeping partner in a new venture. With them came Richard Knowles Spencer (who had married their sister Martha three years earlier), to carry on business as Stewart Brothers and Spencer. Ebenezer was head partner and though there is no record of any capital being put in by Halley or Knowles, the profits were to be shared equally by the three. Old established oil and cake mills were acquired and re-opened at Branbridges, a hamlet close to the village of East Peckham, sited on the Medway four miles east of Tonbridge and about twelve miles south of Rochester. The river and its tributaries, flowing in big curves through attractive countryside, powered a number of mills in the vicinity.[1]

In 1870, when the S.B. and S. partners began making cattle cake, Ebenezer put in his younger brother Josiah as a junior partner in Dickeson and Stewart, he himself (until 1899) remaining a sleeping partner with a fifth share of the profits. A letter introducing the new cattle food to farmers explained that they would produce only pure oil cake, although 'this will mean we relinquish the high profit which is gained by makers of the adulterated article'. Confidence in the better product was justified by a demand which soon led them to set up stands in the markets at Maidstone, Ashford, Tonbridge and Tunbridge Wells. Martha and Knowles went to live at Branbridges. Not long after Ebenezer joined them and, as already noticed, Alexander and Ann Kezia made their retirement home there also. To a certain extent Branbridges replaced Palmer House as the family centre for a few years till the deaths of the parents, and of Martha in August 1875, shattered the circle.

At forty, Ebenezer had married in January 1875 and chosen to live in East Croydon. From no-one in the Stewart family did his bride, Mary Ann Betts, receive a warmer welcome than from Halley's Jane. When the engagement was announced in 1874 Jane wrote to her, recalling that Ebenezer had spent part of his holiday with them when she and Halley enjoyed

[1] Donald Maxwell in his *Unknown Kent* (Bodley Head, 1921) describes his explorations of the Medway and says of this area: 'Through two locks to Branbridges, and then open country which abounds in woods and innumerable tributary brooks.'

their honeymoon stay at Dunoon and Rothesay. 'Very many thoughts and prayers surround you and Ebe (pronounced "Ebbie") which cannot fail to bring a rich blessing,' she went on. 'I anticipate, too, much true, sisterly, loving intercourse with you. I feel that Ebe's wife could not be less to me than my very dear sister and my most intimate friend.' Halley was appointed one of the trustees of the marriage settlement which settled upon Ebenezer's wife, and upon any children of the marriage, the money she had inherited from her father, and it is on record that the income from this increased under Halley's management. He and Ebenezer were in close and constant contact all their lives, and a particularly happy memory for them was of the holiday spent together in 1882 when Rome, Florence and Naples were visited. There was also a strong and lasting friendship between Jane and Ebenezer, founded on their common affection for and loyalty to Halley.

Ere this, Jane and Halley had found the need for new premises for their growing school and family more and more pressing. In July 1872 they moved into Beaufort House, a four-storey house built to Halley's specification in St Leonard's at the corner of Chapel Park Road. But all too soon they outgrew even these new quarters, and in 1879 moved to Park Mansion, again built to Halley's wishes. It included a gymnasium—the first in the town—and had a charming garden and vinery. From here he would set out to visit, to speak, and to attend to affairs. His preaching now took him, however, in a different direction, for in November 1873 Halley had resigned the pastorate of Croft Chapel to become minister at the Caledonian Road chapel in Islington, an imposing building in classical style with a pillared portico. His school friend Henry Allon had himself spent some of the years of his earlier ministry at Islington, and with Palmer House close by, Halley was back in familiar haunts. Here he ministered until 1877.

He did not meanwhile deny his help to the Croft congregation when he could give it, and in September 1876 was presented with an inscribed silver trowel to mark his laying of the foundation stone of a new brick building to replace the old wooden premises which the church had outgrown. The new chapel cost £3,000 and Halley was one of the driving forces behind the fund-raising efforts. For some years he had been secretary of the Ministerial Association of Hastings and St Leonard's, and a testimonial from his Nonconformist colleagues, presented when he left for London, spoke of his 'punctual businesslike management of their affairs and the uniform geniality of his intercourse'.

Left without a pastor, Croft Chapel had the services for eighteen months of Halley's brother John, a year his junior, who was principal of the University School, Hastings. John was another member of the Stewart family to transfer from London to the South Coast, and some of the scholars from Palmer House followed him to complete their education under his care. As another stalwart of Dissent, John was the founder of Congregationalism in nearby Bexhill, where he made his home at 'Heatherdune' in 1886 and began to hold services in a marquee on his lawn. In 1887, the Queen's jubilee year, he helped build Victoria Hall, and continued as pastor until 1896, when increasing school commitments at Hastings led to his resignation. George, the older brother, succeeded him, and under his leadership the present Congregational church in London Road was built in 1897.

3. PULPIT TO POLITICS

POLITICALLY, Halley's fighting spirit was further roused when the Liberals lost the 1874 General Election (Hastings, incidentally, was the only constituency in Sussex which the Conservatives did not win) and Gladstone temporarily retired from public life. He missed his leader's 'marvellous activity and unequalled mastery' (as he put it), and always remembered with pride his journey to Blackheath to represent the Hastings Liberals when Gladstone was welcomed back into the arena in 1876. It was about this time that Halley decided he must leave the ministry for politics. He could not keep politics out of the pulpit, saying of religion that it was not worth a brass farthing unless it dominated the political sphere. Official Congregationalism did not take exactly the same view, but Halley—more independent than any Independent—would not be silenced. Unless the religious teachers helped enlighten their fellow citizens, who all had a duty to influence the law-makers, they were leaving it to wicked men to do it.

It was no light-hearted decision to give up the ministry, but the strain of journeying to the chapel from Hastings was beginning to tell on his health. Moreover, Halley was increasingly convinced that he could do more for the working classes from a political platform than from a chapel pulpit. However, Congregationalism still had his active support. His loyalty and service to it were given freely and fully throughout his long life, and involved at various times being a member of the council and of the finance committee of the English Congregational Church Aid Society, a manager of the Pastors' Retiring Fund, treasurer of the Sussex Congregational Union, and treasurer of the Sussex Congregational Widows' Fund. A testimonial presented in October 1877 at the end of Halley's four years at Islington wished for him a complete restoration of health. It records the achievements of those four years—the extinction of a heavy debt that had burdened the church for twenty years, the honour and esteem it now enjoyed in the denomination, the possibilities of greater usefulness now opened before it, and the 'wisdom and tenderness of your pulpit ministrations, the fitness of your instruction and comfort, and your permanent influence for good.'

Freed from church responsibilities, Halley now had more time and thought for political campaigning. In 1877 he gave rein to a new ambition—to start a local newspaper to back the cause of Liberalism and of social and religious liberty, and to offer competition to the *Hastings Observer*. He achieved this by purchasing an interest in Daniel and Company, a local firm of printers, who then produced the *Hastings and St Leonard's Times* which Halley founded and edited. It had special feature articles on Hastings as well as local news and the political articles which gave great scope to Halley's own pen. Some Tory advertisers boycotted the paper and sometimes Halley's reporters were banned from Tory functions. To the *Times* editor this was only more grist to the local political mill as he trounced the Tories for their dread of freedom in speech and in print.

In the campaign leading to the April 1880 General Election, Halley added to his experience the gruelling labour involved in being honorary election agent to the Liberal candidates in East Sussex. 'I half killed myself over it for I had to speak every night at least once.' The Liberal Party was swept back into power but in Hastings, where there were two seats, a Tory topped the poll and a Liberal came second. Even more shameful to Halley was the fact that the election cost the previous Liberal Member his seat after ten years in Parliament. Halley, who had published costly special supplements in the *Times* carrying full reports of the campaign, wrote that the election had demonstrated the power of the Tory paper and the need which led him to found a Liberal organ. He pleaded for support from readers, subscribers and advertisers to ensure a strong Liberal press as one of the party's mightiest weapons.

He spoke as well as wrote. The Hastings Liberal Association ran lectures on issues of the day and Halley's platform technique was seen here to advantage, for his strong sense of justice and truth, combined with understanding and humour, made him an obvious choice as speaker. There was no lack of topics. Gladstone was grappling with the Irish question. Relations with the Boers were difficult, and the need for reform at home offered room for endless and vigorous examination. As he campaigned on platform and on paper, Halley attained a reputation far beyond Hastings. He was not content merely to speak and write; he offered active service too. Before long he had become a founder member of the National Liberal Club, and belonged to the National Liberal Federation (Birmingham), the London and Home Counties Liberal Union executive, the Leaseholders Enfranchisement Association Council, and the Rochester Liberal 300.

Mention of Rochester is a reminder that it was now the most important place name in the Stewart family. At Branbridges the oil cake business had developed so rapidly that thought had to be given to enlarged production and wider marketing facilities. A water wheel powered the mill machinery, but as demand grew and improved equipment became necessary, the decision was taken to move to Rochester, not more distant than a dozen miles and their nearest point on the coast. Here new mills were built in 1879-80 at a cost of £50,000, linked on the one hand with shipping and on the other hand with the railway and giving opportunity for considerable expansion. Their crushing capacity was 750 tons of seed per week and before long they were working continuously day and night. The premises at Branbridges were sold, and Ebenezer and Knowles both set up new homes at Rochester. Branbridges was not forgotten, however, for the annual outings of the workmen in the earlier years after the move often had this rural retreat as their rendezvous, with Sutton Valence among other alternatives in the lovely Kent countryside.

Halley must have found in the Rochester development much to interest his active brain. Reminiscing to a Toc H audience which met at his house in Harpenden fifty years later, he said he discovered his aptitude for business as a young bank clerk, became a sleeping partner in his brother's business, and eventually took the helm.

After his solid political apprenticeship in Sussex, Halley began to feel he should go further and seek a seat in Parliament. In December 1883 he sold the *Hastings and St Leonard's Times* to Mr J. Macer Wright, a fellow Liberal. It had contributed to his reputation but certainly not to his pocket, possibly because its business side was not his first consideration. In fact the *Times* losses cost him £1,000 in each of the five years he owned it.

Halley would no doubt have been glad to be in Parliament to represent a constituency near home, and there were hopes of an invitation from Rochester. However, in the Spring of 1884 he agreed to make a topical speech at Boston, Lincolnshire, in support of a friend, Mr (later Sir) William Ingram, who had been chosen as a Liberal candidate. The fact that Boston would need a second candidate also weighed with him, but he determined that this should not inhibit his plain speaking when he stood in the Corn Exchange on May 31st. The Bill to give the vote to men of practically all classes was going through Parliament, and Halley argued that the growth of the Press was making everyone more politically conscious and responsible. He thanked Mr Gladstone for making a cheap Press possible, so that a million-and-a-half copies were now in circulation, bringing a newspaper within the reach of every working man.

In a speech which went on for ninety minutes but seemed only half as long, Halley conquered Boston. In this initial exercise in wooing a new constituency he ranged over many topics, his conviction and ability, and his clear reasoning expressed in faultless phrasing, deciding them forthwith that this newcomer was the obvious colleague for Mr Ingram. As the public sat under the spell of his words, what kind of man did they see? A member of the Boston audience paints the portrait thus—'a countenance combining power with character, with a broad high forehead, lips showing firmness and earnestness, eyes keen and searching yet often filled with kindly light. When speaking, the play of his features is fine and his manner commanding. He will make his mark as a legislator . . .'.

Boston Liberals were not slow in asking Halley to

be their second candidate. Among the matters he emphasized on accepting was the point that, despite his reverence for Mr Gladstone, he could never be anything but an independent member of the Liberal Party. He spoke plainly, too, of the bribery and corruption which had been associated with Boston. He sought assurances that the Liberals would not tarnish his name by associating it with anything that had taken place there. 'I should feel the task altogether too great if my seat were purchased by fraudulent money gifts to constituents who were recording their votes for that price. I do not want a seat in the House of Commons unless I have behind me the unbought approval of the constituency which has asked me to fight its battle.'

If Halley had needed anything to bring his political ardour to white heat at the start of his association with Boston, he surely found it in the national agitation against the House of Lords because of their rejection of the Franchise Bill. On July 21st he watched from a window of the National Liberal Club as 30,000 people marched to Hyde Park to link up with 20,000 already there to protest against the Lords. He joined the demonstrators and then went straight to Boston to speak at another Liberal gathering. 'The nation is but half franchised. It must be completely franchised, and the House of Lords must be set in order ere this thing is done,' was how he summed up this explosive national situation.

Halley went up and down the constituency speaking to the voteless men of Lincolnshire, and at both Liberal and Tory meetings the question of the Lords was thrashed out. The Tories realized that Halley threatened their cause, and disparaged the effectiveness of his speeches by sneering at this 'verbal pyrotechny'. But the county knew what it wanted and at a joint rally in Lincoln from all the divisions, 50,000 demonstrated in favour of the extended franchise. Halley did not confine himself to Boston but helped the campaign wherever he could. At Stoke, in the Potteries, he escaped with bruises when the platform collapsed. What made this meeting even more memorable was that his fellow victims included Joseph Chamberlain and Jesse Collings, whose efforts put the first Allotment Act on the statute book.

Prosperity at the Rochester mills had made it possible for Halley to pursue his widespread political activities in security. After fifteen years the partners had built up a business of considerable magnitude, but in the autumn of 1884, eclipsing the strain of the political agitations in which he immersed himself, came a sudden and unexpected disaster. The mills were destroyed by fire. The chilling news reached Halley at his home in Hastings at 10.30 p.m. on November 15th. At once he and Knowles set off for Rochester, driving through the night and changing horses where they could. As they neared the town the glare in the sky confirmed only too well the dreadful news. They reached the mill at 5 a.m. to realize that the flames had reduced the business to a ruin. At the mill worked 150 men. 'I was consumed with the awful sense of the tragedy of life as I considered the fate of these men compelled to join the ranks of the unemployed,' wrote Halley afterwards.

The blaze became known as 'The Great Fire of Rochester' and was fully described in the *Rochester and Chatham Journal*. Taking a Sunday evening stroll about nine o'clock, a resident saw a light flickering at the top of the mill building housing a 300,000 gallon tank of linseed oil, and immediately alerted the mill manager, Mr Lee. When the horse-drawn fire engine arrived and hoses were connected to the main, the water pressure was negligible, and the manual engine was called for pumping by hand. Mill hands worked like galley slaves to salvage oil cake from store and to run off linseed oil from the blazing tank into barrels, but at 6 a.m. the tank itself exploded, showering blazing oil over the whole of the mill premises and setting them all alight. Not till the dockyard sent two powerful steam fire engines to the scene was the blaze finally brought under control about 9 a.m.

Halley reckoned the firm's loss by damage was at least £60,000. It was a stunning blow. Yet on the day following the fire he was honouring engagements to speak on Liberal platforms at Alford and Spalding. The *Spalding Guardian* paid willing tribute to 'a man of high social position who, in the middle of a time of great anxiety and mental strain after such a calamity as the fire at his mills, has so much regard for the righteousness of the cause he espouses that he keeps three appointments a distance from home'. The following Sunday Halley preached from the words in Ecclesiastes 3: 'A time to weep and a time to laugh; a time to mourn and a time to dance; a time to get and a time to lose.' Yet despite his faith he was sorely tried, and for some months the only income he and his family had was from the girls' school. Jane's calmness, her unshaken confidence in her husband, her steadfast encouragement and her careful management were at this time a special source of strength.

Soon after the fire both Ebenezer and Knowles moved for a time into smaller houses in Rochester. It is tribute in itself to the partners that new mills, planned to include greatly-desired extensions and improvements, were completed and operating two years later. But things were not quite the same. All had gone well from the start of the enterprise in 1869–70 up to the fire of 1884, steady progress and increasing profits marking the period. But after the mills were burned down, the firm could no longer afford to carry a sleeping partner.

While the others supervised operations at the new mills, Halley therefore began specializing in their financial management. Much of the success of the business depended on the judicious buying of linseed as the main raw material, and Halley watched the markets and did this essential part of the work from the London office with enviable foresight and soundness of judgment. His brother's need of help was all the greater, too, because of an interest in a chemical business in Wales. As managing director, this made considerable claims upon his time. Halley's own commitments precluded continuous contact with the mills and he was obliged to rely heavily on correspondence for detailed news, for there were then no telephones or dictaphones in common use to help busy executives. Ebenezer's family life was therefore often interrupted by the need to compile long and closely-written reports for the post. It is still remembered as a demanding chore but he was adamant about the need to do it despite entreaties from the domestic circle.

Ebenezer's belief in Halley's business ability was, in fact, so amply justified that it was not long before a new deed of partnership was entered into under which Halley was made senior partner, relieving Ebenezer and drawing the largest share of the profits.

4. INTO PARLIAMENT

HALLEY continued his active political campaigning, though during the winter of 1884 he found himself unexpectedly out of the Boston division when it became a one-member constituency. South Lincolnshire was divided into the three Parliamentary divisions of Stamford, Spalding and Sleaford, and both Stamford and Spalding invited him to stand. Halley accepted the latter invitation at a Spalding mass meeting on March 30, 1885, after he had been pressed to do so at a series of meetings throughout the division. The warmth of the welcome and support he received was a tonic suited to his need after the fateful fire and the door closing against him—albeit most regretfully—at Boston. That warmth, heated afresh at the fires of his own passion and conviction, Halley passed back to his constituents, liking most of all to teach the labourers what Liberal principles meant and how by their newly-gained votes they could help to put them into practice.

The next General Election was fixed for the autumn of 1885. It was Halley's first candidature, and in it he had the enthusiastic support of Richard Winfrey as worker and then agent. Winfrey was the son of Richard Francis Winfrey of Long Sutton, and was holidaying at home from London, where he was a fully qualified chemist with John Bell and Company in Oxford Street. Since 1882 Winfrey had been leader of the Liberal movement in the St James Parliamentary Debating Society, and back in the Spalding Division he quickly came under the power of Halley's eloquence and drive. He spent his holiday in supporting him, and then decided to forsake his position in London in order to promote his cause in the General Election.

For Winfrey, then only twenty-seven, it was a serious step to take. Halley was forty-seven. He honoured Richard Francis Winfrey and was often his guest when in the constituency, while with Richard he began a friendship which was to persist up to his death and was in due course to embrace another Winfrey generation, Richard's son Richard Pattinson. The two enthusiasts were indefatigable as they worked for a Liberal success in Spalding. One of their activities was to journey together through all the parishes around Spalding and South Holland, their survey revealing, among other things, that there were less than 500 acres devoted to allotments and no smallholdings at all. They did not forget this.

Opposing them in the Conservative interest was the sitting member, the Hon Murray Finch-Hatton of Haverholme Priory, son of the Earl of Winchilsea, heir to considerable estates in Lincolnshire and elsewhere, and both by background and ability a formidable opponent. Halley did not underestimate the forces against him—and these included the fact that throughout the division many of the labourers who should be voting for the first time, and to whom he felt he could make a special appeal, were not qualified through inefficient compilation of the new electoral registers. In addition, Halley had to speak out against the farmers and landowners who harshly made it clear that their men would have to choose between voting the master's way or losing their jobs. To the labourers he emphasized that the ballot was genuinely secret; to their bosses he uttered the threat of invoking the new Corrupt Practices Act. Indeed, at least one farmer found himself before the magistrates at Halley's instigation, and this led to more subtle ways of persuasion when farmers began to invite their men round for a drink, smoke, and a harmless chat on politics generally.

It was a robust campaign. Halley's known Radical views provided the Tories with extra ammunition to throw back at him, and he was abused over Disestablishment, Sunday School work, land for the people and other serious matters. Exposing their distortions gave Halley openings to drive home his real views. But silly slanders about his domestic life at Hastings he did not stoop to answer. When the Tories, anxious to put on an impressive demonstration, brought train-loads of ticket-holders to a Corn Exchange mass meeting, more than a thousand outraged working men unable to get in developed an ugly mood. Halley was having an evening off but he seized the opportunity to speak to the turbulent crowd from a wagon, quietened them by the sheer force of his personality, and gained many more converts.

The labourers rallied to Halley's championship of their right to hold allotments, and when Jesse Collings came down to speak he went with Halley and Richard Winfrey to Long Sutton, where a big demonstration in support of his recent Act led a little later to the release of charity lands for allotments. It was a happiness for the busy candidate when Jane came to Spalding for a week to see how the Fen folk lived, and there was a special welcome for her when she went to a meeting at Butterwick. With wifely discretion, she normally eluded the limelight at her husband's public functions, but on this evening made a short impromptu speech after three cheers had been roared out in her honour. Halley never forgot his delight at hearing her speak.

Mrs Stewart was in Spalding for election day, December 2, 1885, and with Halley drove round the polling stations in a decorated carriage drawn by a pair of greys. Richard Winfrey recalls that she wore a beautiful blue dress for the occasion with bonnet to match. They returned deeply disturbed at seeing masters standing at the doors of so many of the polling stations as their men came to vote, and letters from labourers received after the election confirmed that there were many who voted against their consciences. Halley persuaded the National Liberal Club to investigate some of these cases, but redress in the courts was difficult to obtain from Tory magistrates.

Finch-Hatton was returned with 4,658 votes, only 78 ahead of Halley Stewart, and this convinced him that in a fair fight he would have won. From the balcony of the Red Lion Hotel Halley spoke of the campaign. 'I have had to fight soup tickets, I have had to fight quarter and half pounds of tea, and I have had to fight coal tickets as well as Finch-Hatton. I have had to fight the terror of Parsondom, politics on Sundays as well as on weekdays, and the undue influence of local farmers. I should have received the votes of hundreds of willing supporters if they had had the courage of their convictions. . . .'

Halley was sure that though he had been denied the harvest, he had sown the seed of a Liberal victory for someone in the future. When he and Jane left later that night for home, their carriage was dragged to the station by working men followed by a crowd of 500 supporters, mostly labourers and their wives. Village folk thronged the platform and Halley shook hands with nearly all of them as the engine driver moved off at slow speed. It was an unforgettable moment. 'In the hour of defeat, they cast no word of reproach' he recalled in a speech at Spalding more than forty years later. By then so much that he had fought for had become commonplace—freedom for men to speak their own minds, freedom for men to till their own land, freedom for men to vote according to their own consciences. 'When I came to Spalding the very dress of the agricultural labourer was a witness to the disparity of his condition. But who can tell now, when sitting in a railway carriage, whether he is next to a millionaire's or a labourer's wife?'

Richard Winfrey had been in the thick of the fight with Halley, sharing the toil, the wounds and the heartbreak. Halley's first duty at home was to send an expression of his deep gratitude to one with whom he hoped there would be a long friendship. In his letter from Park Mansion dated December 4th he wrote: 'Your share of the anxiety has been greater than mine. I know what it is to be an honorary election agent, as well as a candidate. I have served Liberalism in both capacities, and I do not hesitate to say that my responsibilities and anxieties when I worked East Sussex as honorary agent in 1880 were greater than during my candidature in Spalding. The constituency will never know how much of the measure of success we achieved was due to your energy and self-sacrifice.' Thus gratefully and affectionately did the older man acknowledge his debt to the younger, and deeply it touched the latter—perhaps more than any of the many letters that were to reach him during his own years of immersion in politics and business.

Halley paid his own election expenses and shared the cost with the other candidate of providing polling stations, ballot boxes and clerks. Candidates had to bear this financial burden till after the General Election of 1906, when Winfrey—who had first sought with success to reduce the election bill in 1885 and was himself by then a Member—led a deputation to the Prime Minister, Sir Henry Campbell-Bannerman, asking for the law to be changed. The empty house used at Long Sutton as an election committee room was opened on January 16, 1886, as a Liberal Club, with Richard Winfrey as secretary.

In Parliament, Gladstone seemed safe with eighty-six Irish Home Rulers returned to help ensure a Liberal majority. But when he outlined his scheme of self-government for Ireland, this bold attempt to settle one of the most urgent problems of the day divided his party. In May 1886 his Home Rule Bill was defeated in the House by thirty votes in spite of his impassioned advocacy. Gladstone decided to take the issue to the country, and in June 1886—only six months after being returned to power—the Liberal Party faced another election. Meanwhile Halley, reacting to an unusually cold spring and the after-effects of his strenuous campaign in the Fens, had been seriously ill with influenza. As early as February, Spalding Division Liberals had started a fighting fund for the next election. At the Corn Exchange in March, after a knife and fork tea, Halley had been presented with a large framed testimonial on vellum, recording the appreciation of the 4,500 electors who voted for him in December 1885 and expressing the hope that he would lead their cause to victory on the next occasion.

On June 22, 1886, Halley started campaigning. Finch-Hatton was again on the other side, though a throat infection prevented him speaking, and the defective register of 1885 was still in force. The Liberals were bewildered by the way Home Rule had divided their leading politicians, though Halley's own views on the Irish were clear. 'These men are asking for themselves only what we in Spalding are asking for ourselves, the right of self-government, for a return to the self-government they once enjoyed but which was wrung from them by trickery and fraud.' He argued, too, that if the Irish had land of their own they might not over-run Lincolnshire farms at harvest, working for low sums to which English wages were all too often pegged.

But he could not stem the tide running against the party. On July 10th, less than three weeks after starting his campaign, Halley polled 4,273 votes, with Finch-Hatton increasing his majority over him to 288. Liberal abstentions were blamed for this by Winfrey, who again acted as agent. Though bitterly disappointed, and very anxious about what would happen in Ireland, Halley's departure from Spalding was again a triumph. 'At this very moment,' he told the crowd after the declaration of the poll, 'we are preparing for the next election and whoever comes to Spalding to lift up the Liberal standard, I shall be here to give a helping hand.'

With Lord Salisbury in power, the Conservatives prepared to reinforce coercive measures to quell the troubles in Ireland. Feeling in the country ran high. One hundred and fifty thousand men marched to Hyde Park to protest, and on April 21, 1887, Halley, writing to Richard Winfrey, was glad to hear that there was to be a protest at Long Sutton the next day against what he called a Crimes rather than Coercion Bill. Winfrey had reason to remember that occasion. Stung by an insult to his father, who was presiding at an overflow meeting and was called a liar by a Tory, he waited to the end and then demanded an apology. In the ensuing argument he knocked the man's top hat over his eyes.

Halley did not approve of such conduct but Winfrey fully publicised the affair in the *Spalding Guardian*. (He had gone into business as owner and editor in April). As a result he was taken to court and ordered to pay £20 damages for assault. The resentment stirred up against the Tories by this vindictive prosecution was, however, to bear a quick return in a harvest of Liberal votes. For on June 11th Lord Winchilsea died. Finch-Hatton succeeded to the title, and a by-election in Spalding became necessary. Winfrey at once wired Halley Stewart, and caught the next train to London to discuss the situation with Arnold Morley, the Liberal Chief Whip, and with Francis Schnadhorst, one of the party managers. Morley insisted that the names of certain important ex-Cabinet Ministers who had lost their seats should go before the Spalding Association, but Schnadhorst agreed with Winfrey that Halley Stewart was the most likely person to swing the division behind Gladstone and Home Rule.

The Association's loyalty to Halley led to his acceptance for the third time of the challenge to fight. He dared, they noticed, to risk defeat again for them, and in return the Association took over liability for his expenses, with help from the Party in London. London, in fact, focused its attention on this struggle. Was its outcome to be another blow for Gladstone, another reverse for the Party, another rejection of Home Rule? Or was the tide on the turn? Halley had begun his campaign before the Tories had chosen a candidate. One of the largest landowners in

South Lincolnshire was Lady Willoughby, whose daughter had married Rear Admiral George Tryon of Bulwick Hall, Northamptonshire. He had landed at Plymouth only three days before the election campaign started, and agreed to stand for Spalding. He had had no experience of party politics and electioneering found him out of his element, but there were formidable forces on his side—the power of the local aristocracy, traditional Conservative influence, and his own Service reputation among them.

The Royal Navy in the closing years of the old Queen's reign represented the ultimate in nineteenth century power politics, and Tryon—big, bluff and bearded, with a rugged but dynamic personality and courage to match—was the country's beau ideal of a sea dog. Serving with distinction in a navy which had been virtually at peace for three-quarters of a century, he boldly advocated and practised unorthodox methods, and may have seen membership of the Commons as a means towards achieving further naval reform. The honour of a KCB for Tryon was announced during the election. The Government sent Ministerial speakers to support him. Irish Members of Parliament came to speak for Halley and for Home Rule, including the famous T. P. O'Connor, who represented a Liverpool constituency and had just started the London evening paper *The Star*. Another Home Ruler was his namesake, 'Long John' O'Connor, MP—very tall, very Irish, very excitable and very popular. There was trouble on both sides over certain names on the electors' list; and Winfrey's assault case was heard. All were unusual aspects of a strange election.

Halley urged and argued the Irish cause, pleading that they should have a Parliament for domestic affairs with London controlling Imperial affairs, and that this should be conceded 'graciously in the hour of English strength and not grudgingly in an hour of weakness'. Part of the hot summer evening on the night before the election was spent by Halley in the bar of the White Hart Hotel talking to Tory tenant farmers, 'preparing them for the inevitable' and then shaking hands with them all. With him on his polling day tour on July 1st went his eldest son Reginald, now nineteen. To the Conservatives the issue was never in serious doubt, and in such a traditionally Tory area there seemed little reason for Sir George Tryon to question their confidence in his return. A carriage and greys, with postillions and outriders in pink, were ready for his triumphal tour the next day. A hearse was to follow as a sign of the Liberal candidate's final rejection, with wreaths of red paper made by ladies of the Primrose League. 'In memory of Halley Stewart and the Liberal cause' was the message printed on black-edged cards ready for distribution.

Counting the votes started at ten o'clock the next day and Admiral Tryon came to the Corn Exchange to hear the result about an hour later. He found Halley nervously anxious as he waited. Well he might be, for no Liberal had won a contested election in South Lincolnshire since the Reform Bill was passed in 1832. How triumphant a victory for Halley, therefore, and how stunning a blow for the Tories when the Admiral found the electorate had rejected him by 747 votes—4,363 to the Liberal 5,110 after a record poll in what was looked upon throughout the country as a test election.

To his supporters roaring and cheering in ecstasy outside the Corn Exchange Halley spoke in these terms: 'Today we harvest the fruits of three years hard and arduous service and garner a victory for the Liberal Party, for our splendid leader and above all for the cause of justice to our fellow subjects in Ireland. . . . You have shown that you know how to be courageous in defeat. I hope you will now show moderation in victory. Our defeated friends are our fellow townsmen and fellow citizens. Let us show that in our splendid triumph we are worthy to wear the honours we have won.' The defeated candidate was at first unable to gain a hearing from the crowd following their great ovation for the new Member, and when Halley tried to quieten them Sir George would have none of it. Amid the interruptions he asserted that he came before them as an Englishman, and he did not ask for any forbearance—certainly not from his adversary. The crowd broke into fresh uproar at this and the Tory speech ended abruptly.

Bold, arrogant, forthright, capable but unpolitical, Sir George went back to sea, never to stand on a party platform again. In the 1888 manoeuvres he commanded 'enemy' forces which played havoc with the naval squadrons defending England and his name rang through the land. In September 1891 Sir George, now a Vice Admiral, was appointed Commander-in-Chief Mediterranean. In 1893 he went down with his flagship, H.M.S. *Victoria*, which cost £845,000 and was one of the finest and most heavily protected ironclads in the Royal Navy, when it was accidentally rammed by his second-in-command's ship, the *Camperdown*, off Tripoli, on the Syrian coast, on June 22nd. The loss of this ship, with 358 officers and men, in exercises in a dead calm sea stunned the nation. Messages came from heads of state in the old world and the new, and Queen Victoria cancelled a state ball planned for June 23rd. A court martial held on board ship in Malta Harbour laid blame for the tragedy on supposed errors in orders given by Tryon to his fleet, but had Sir George been there to clarify the matter, the court's findings might well have been different.[1] A memorial tablet in Bulwick church, hard by his ancestral home in Northamptonshire, bears a bearded likeness and recalls that he was wounded in the trenches before Sebastopol before going on to achieve a world-wide reputation as seaman, strategist and tactician. Such was the man whom Halley defeated.

After a celebration lunch at the Red Lion and much speech-making from the hotel balcony, Reginald thanked the crowd for the honour shown to his father, and then together they started for home. Working men escorted their carriage through cheering crowds to the station. At Hastings, the train halted by a platform ablaze with lights, with the bands of the Junior Liberals and of the Volunteers playing 'See, the Conquering Hero comes'. Then a torchlight procession escorted them to Park Mansion where the young ladies of the school hung out of the bedroom windows to join in the shouts of welcome. Back at Spalding cards were printed for distribution giving the voting figures. It bore two illustrations— the 'Cock that crows when the battle's done', in blue, and the 'Cock that crows ere the work is done', in red and tipped over on its back. Many a card was stuffed into the letterboxes of the Conservatives to rub salt into the wounds received that day, and one such card survives to this day in Richard Winfrey's papers.

[1] The circumstances are fully discussed in *Admirals in Collision*, by Richard Hough; Hamish Hamilton, 1959.

5. THE BUSY MEMBER

PRESS, public and private comment throughout the country all agreed that the Spalding victory had given the Conservatives a nasty jolt. Morley and Schnadhorst both wrote to praise Winfrey for his arduous exertions, and Mr Gladstone made a point of coming to the House to join in the Opposition's crashing cheers as Halley walked its length on taking his seat in the Commons. This was on the Monday following the election. Already it had made political history. The Spalding victory gave new life to the Liberal Party in Parliament and outside. Gladstone, on a private visit to Norfolk, arranged for the train to stop at Spalding so that he could personally congratulate Halley and his supporters on their triumph.

How did Halley strike his contemporaries? Friendship and comradeship do not distort this portrait of him drawn at the time in the *Sheffield Independent* by T. P. O'Connor: 'He has thought out all the great questions of the day thoroughly and his conclusions, though fierce and extreme, are always backed up by clear and logical argument. He has striking features. His face is strong and rugged. The general impression is one of robust manliness. His eyes are blue, bright and restless, and they indicate a character consumed by strong conviction and a fierce enthusiasm for humanity. His victory is certainly largely due to the personal magnetism he has exercised over the constituency of Spalding. His activity is stupendous.'

Such a man could never be content to go with the crowd. He cast three votes in his first two days in the House. The first two were for the Liberals, the third for the Government—in support of a man's right to speak on his own behalf in a witness box. To critics he replied that his votes were for what was essentially liberal, not necessarily for party Liberalism. The new Member's influence was quickly sought in support of Liberal candidates at other by-elections, and his aid was freely acknowledged in victories at Coventry, at Ayr, and in Yorkshire. Before the year was out he made his maiden speech in the House on the Conservative Allotment Bill. The support given in the Fens to Halley's advocacy of land for the labourers had, in fact, alerted the Government to the need for action. As Mr Gladstone himself pointed out: 'The Spalding election, like a flash of lightning, conveyed an illumination of the Ministerial minds, and they became aware that it was of vast importance to have a Bill upon allotments.'

Halley and his friends were disappointed in the Bill but he spoke in favour of it as a small though sadly feeble start to what they wanted. In due course it became law, but laid down so many conditions that its practical ineffectiveness seemed assured. During the winter of 1887–88 he explained the provisions of the Act in meetings in the Fens, preaching the rights of the labourer from the text: 'The husbandman that laboureth must be first partaker of the fruits.' He pushed home the point. Who was to be the first? Not the owner, not the mortgagee, not the State, not the tax-gatherer, not the county, not the ratepayer, not the idle occupier of land—but the husbandman, the active farmer toiling together with the labourer.

Ten acres of land were eventually made available at Whaplode but this was derisory, with sixteen hundred applicants in the division. So Richard Winfrey initiated allotment clubs in many parishes to

Rev. Halley Stewart the young preacher— a Hastings portrait

Ebenezer Stewart in his late twenties (c. 1864): of Halley's elder brothers the nearest to him by birth, in outlook and in enterprise

Halley Stewart Esq., J.P.

Mrs Halley Stewart

try to get land on a voluntary basis. The Spalding Provident Club soon found a friend in Lord Carrington, who allocated thirty acres on one of his farms. Not only so but he told his tenants: 'Farm as you like, vote as you like, pay when you like.' Such an enlightened move greatly heartened the campaigners and led to the 1889 victory, when the Lincolnshire County Council elections were fought successfully on the allotments issue.

Halley's solicitude for the labourer was but part of his deep and wide concern for all those whose distress and poverty contrasted so painfully with the idleness and riches that marked the age. 'Is it true,' he asked in the House shortly after joining it, 'that there are waifs in London without even a sack to cover them?' The *Lincolnshire Chronicle*, reporting on this query and its sequel, told how a bundle of sacks had been sent to Halley, on each of which was pinned a copy of the question. 'Half a dozen sacks to cover the nakedness of four hundred people,' was the Member's comment. Further to answer his own question, he went early in August to see the homeless sleeping in the squares and under the arches. He set himself to paint the haunting picture on public platforms; he determined to campaign to put it right by private persuasion and open advocacy. He found that forty-five per cent of the population aged over sixty had been or were in the workhouses or dependent on relief, apart from far too many who would rather die than seek shelter within their grim walls.

If it was religion to feed the hungry, to give drink to the thirsty, to clothe the naked and to minister to the sick, it was equally religion—in Halley's mind—to allow the working classes the divine right to work, and to secure for their toil a legitimate reward. He preached: he practised. He had labourers working for him in his own mills—the firm paid the highest wages then known in the trade. Halley's widening experience of life in London showed him also the other side of the coin—the wealth of the rich and the luxury of their social life. But extravagance did not create comfort for the poor. He urged that labour to be good should benefit the community. Better to buy two hundred dresses for £200 than allow one lady to spend that figure on a single dress, was the simple way he expounded his economic faith.

Though, for all his fire and force on the platform, Halley was sometimes rightly criticised for being long-winded, in the House he spoke much more concisely and to great effect. When Percy was once visiting Westminster T. M. Healy, the Irish political leader and MP for Wexford, looked him up and down. 'So you're a son of Halley Stewart,' he said. 'We respect him here. He never trims his sails, and we always know where he stands.' His faithfulness in attendance was in marked contrast to Finch-Hatton's record, and he studied the issues before Parliament with penetrating earnestness. Sir William Harcourt included him when naming three representative Englishmen whose opinions on rural matters were specially worth having. He sat through the all-night sittings, frequently appeared at meetings outside his own constituency, and was heartily glad of the physical and mental relief when Parliament recessed at the end of the summer.

Then came the honour and inspiration of a trip to the United States, chosen to go with Sir John Swinburne and Mr O. V. Morgan to prepare the way for a party of Members who were to present a petition to President Cleveland and Congress, advocating arbitration between the two countries where ordinary diplomacy failed. America, home of many Irish, feted him for his stand on Home Rule and acclaimed him for his Spalding victory. Halley, with the other two, was introduced in the Senate, addressed the Foreign Affairs Committee, and attended sittings of the Upper and Lower Houses of the Virginian State Legislature.

Back home, his energy in visiting his division and speaking in the villages offended the Tories. He must be paid for speaking, they gibed. The inauguration of a women's branch in Spalding of the Liberal Association was another upset for them, but Halley persevered with this development, hoping from it a higher tone in public and political life. Not all the Liberals agreed with him but from Hastings Jane wrote to accept the presidency, glad 'that women of leisure and culture are rousing themselves to grapple with political problems'. There was no apathy to make Halley doubt the value of his village visits. They were usually crowded with supporters of both sides, eager to sing his praises or to shout their scorn. Sometimes too, there were rough-and-tumbles when ruffians were abroad, but Halley more than survived. Richard Winfrey controlled the *Spalding Guardian* and Halley regularly checked it for reports of local events, including his own speeches. As an ex-editor he did not spare his colleague. 'There are some sentences in the report of my speech which are exquisitely amusing, the very opposite of what I said,' he once wrote. 'They are fearfully and wonderfully made. They were so originally. But more so in the paper.'

The two friends carried on a constant correspondence. Winfrey had asked Halley's advice before purchasing the *Guardian*, and Halley, in fact, gave some financial assistance to him at the beginning of the venture, being joined in this by Dr J. T. Crowden, a distinguished London surgeon whose health had led him to a quieter practice in the Spalding countryside, at Gedney Hill. The three originally formed a company with Dr Crowden as secretary, but Winfrey later became sole proprietor. Halley wanted the paper to succeed for Winfrey's sake as well as for the Liberal cause. He knew from his own experience that Liberals did not always match their lip service to the Press with practical support, and felt that Spalding should back the *Guardian* more substantially. At the same time he encouraged Winfrey to deal with blemishes in its pages. 'The paper is badly read and badly put together,' he wrote in August 1887, 'and I must say its original writing has of late been very feeble. . . . Half-a-dozen pen strokes would sometimes put quite an improved complexion on articles and notes spoilt for want of a touch of a master's hand.' The need for this faithful admonition is explained by Richard Winfrey's growing reputation as an election agent since Francis Schnadhorst first noticed his aptitude when Halley was elected. His demands often kept Winfrey out of Spalding for he sought his aid in almost every by-election between 1887 and 1894, the year that Richard Winfrey himself became a candidate.

As his first year in Parliament wore on, Halley's constant journeys and speeches, added to the demands of Parliamentary and business life, steadily took their toll, and on August 14, 1888, he went to Brussels for a holiday. But when the date of a Liberal gathering at Nocton Park was altered and clashed with this, Halley broke into the respite, travelling nearly a thousand miles there and back to keep his promise to speak. How could he ration his engagements? 'I want a rhinoceros skin umbrella to keep off invitations to speak. I have declined four today,' he told Winfrey in a letter on September 23rd. It seemed, however, that he would never learn, for in excusing himself to Winfrey from a Spalding engagement in July 1890, he explained: 'I do not want the impression to get abroad that I am ill; nothing of the kind. I am simply worn out. It was just the same at Easter and at Whitsuntide. But I will not trouble you with all this.'

Halley strove with the rest for a Liberal victory when the Holland Division of Lincolnshire elected its first county council under the 1888 Local Government Act, and January 1889 saw twenty-two Liberals (including Richard Winfrey) voted in against fifteen Conservatives and five Independents. The county Liberals gained office on the question of land for the people, and with agricultural seats being lost to them at almost every by-election, the Conservative Government tried to improve the situation with the Allotments Amendment Act of 1890. This permitted labourers to appeal to their county councils if boards of guardians failed to provide land. With sympathy at that level assured in Holland, allotment acreage increased to a record far beyond anything shown in the ten other counties which succeeded in operating the Act up to the time of the Liberal Small Holdings Act of 1907.

An interesting visit for Halley in July 1889 was with a delegation of Members of Parliament to the Parliamentary Peace Conference in Paris. Later that summer he was with Members on board the troopship Serapis for an inspection tour of the Royal Navy. In the course of this the party were met by Admiral Tryon but there is no record of his feelings on seeing Halley once more at such close quarters. To save wear and tear on their Member, Spalding Division Liberals arranged for other speakers to take some of the meetings, and also made use of a horse-drawn caravan built for mobile accommodation by the Eastern Counties Liberal Federation. It comprised bedroom, dressing room, kitchen and speakers' platform; was named 'Sunrise', and was drawn by a horse called 'Gladstone'. George Nicholls, a young workman who accepted the post of driver-attendant, became principal travelling speaker and in 1906 himself entered Parliament for North Northamptonshire.

In and out of Parliament Halley spoke with great indignation and urgency against the plight of the Irish under Tory tyranny and coercion, and the gaoling of Irish Members of Parliament (twenty-three in twelve months) was an intolerable outrage which he condemned in stinging phrases. Though the country's sympathies were being stirred, it grieved him that 'that occulent force which we call moral indignation has been so latent that the Government has not been swept out of office'. To confirm his assertion that Ireland had become a police state, Halley visited the country to see conditions for himself, being closely watched by the police all the time he was there. Jane was in the party and Halley spoke at fifteen meetings. On his return, he was uncompromisingly critical of the Royal Irish Constabulary—'fomentors of discord and the principal breakers of law and order in Ireland' whose best contribution to quietness would be to stay in their barracks.

During 1890 it seemed certain that the Irish question would bring the Liberals back into office. Certain, that is, until the bleak autumn day when Parnell, leader of the Irish Members, was branded in the Divorce Court on account of adultery with the wife of his friend Captain O'Shea. Goaded by the sharp-edged criticism that poured upon him from friend and foe alike, Parnell's bitter reaction and refusal to retire from the scene smashed the alliance between the Irish and Liberal Parties when victory seemed just around the corner. Parnell died in October 1891, four months after marrying Mrs O'Shea. Halley stood apart from the condemnation. When the divorce action started he declared: 'Home Rule is not a personal question. We shall not feel that Home Rule is more good if Mr Parnell's virtue is lauded to the skies, and we shall not feel that Home Rule is a failure if one man is proved to be human in his erring and weakness as well as courageous and consistent.' But for the time being in the country and in the Commons, Home Rule was practically a dead duck.

Other matters gave scope for Halley's outspoken views. In the New Year of 1891 he voted for the Government's Religious Disabilities Bill which would, among other things, permit a Roman Catholic to be Lord Chancellor. How could he, with all his hatred of religious bigotry, vote otherwise? He was criticized for this, and came under fire also for supporting the move to pay Members of Parliament £300 a year. He saw it as a means whereby working men could sit in Parliament and there plead the cause of their kith and kin. 'One of my chief disqualifications in representing you,' Halley told his Spalding supporters, 'is not that I am too poor but that I am too rich. Every principle that I advocate in the House and in this constituency tends to make me a poorer man, because I know that by the incidence of unjust legislation in the past I have what I ought not to possess and you are deprived of your right, and it is my mission in life to try to bring it to you.'

Jane was still carrying on her school, and the oil cake mills were in full swing with Halley as chief partner. When Parliament was sitting Halley usually stayed in London at the National Liberal Club, going back to St Leonard's to spend the weekends with his family. He could devote little time to local affairs and had the disappointment of seeing the editor of the *Hastings and St Leonard's Times*, which he had founded in 1877 and sold in 1883, turn against him. This was in 1889, when in a January letter to Richard Winfrey he begs him not to publish in the *Spalding Guardian* a copy of a letter signed J. Macer Wright. Halley explained that Macer Wright had bought the Hastings paper from him and had since made it a neutral paper under a joint directorate of Tories and Liberals. This had compromised Hastings Liberalism, for Macer Wright was vice-president of the Liberal Association and a good political speaker. Because he had opposed Liberal Town Council candidates and made the paper independent, the Liberal Committee begged Halley to stand for the presidency to prevent Macer Wright taking office. There was no-one else strong enough to beat him, so he reluctantly agreed. Meanwhile Halley's name was smeared in the Hastings and other papers, including the *Lincolnshire Herald*, but he refrained from any reply or self-vindication. This came a little later in full measure at the Public Hall where 800 people voted Halley in as Hastings Liberal Association president, with Macer Wright attracting only eight votes.

Another local honour came in 1891 with Halley's appointment as a Justice of the Peace for East Sussex. He was sworn in at the Midsummer Quarter Sessions at Lewes on June 30th, an attack of influenza and a holiday trip in May having delayed this formality. The holiday was spent aboard a 150-ton barge which Halley had had fitted up as a yacht, some of his children going with him. Investigating the shortage of magistrates in Lincolnshire had led him to deplore the fact that they were entirely recruited from one class. He wanted to see justice administered by those who appreciated that 'five shillings and costs' meant an entire week's income to working men, and he wanted to see Radicals and Nonconformists among their number. Halley knew that such views would scarcely commend him to the authorities, but his appointment was a result of Richard Winfrey's suggestion to the Hon Arthur Brand, for whom he was election agent at Wisbech, a division in the Fens adjoining Spalding. Brand was the third son of the first Viscount Hampden, former Speaker of the House of Commons, and it was Lord Hampden who wrote to tell Halley he had nominated him for the Commission of the Peace.

In 1890 Lloyd George became Member for Caernarvon at one of a number of Liberal by-election victories which put the Party in good heart for the General Election of November 15, 1892. In Spalding, Halley found himself with a fresh Tory opponent in Harry Pollock, a Liberal until the Home Rule split and a City solicitor and financier who scattered subscriptions with an all-too-lavish generosity. Halley stood by the attitude which he had made clear back in 1885—that he would be judged on his political merits and not as a general relieving officer. 'If the Spalding seat is to be put up for auction I am not in the field to make an offer for it,' he declared. For the summer and autumn Halley occupied Westbourne House in Spalding, glad to have with him there Jane and his daughter and also Percy, with Reginald later. Aged twenty, Percy had left the Royal High School in Edinburgh and was having his first experience of business. He was still a schoolboy, lodging with a United Presbyterian minister, when he danced round a bonfire in the manse garden in 1887 to celebrate his father's dramatic victory over Admiral Tryon. He never forgot that the bonfire burned the minister's best cherry tree. Now he came to help his father win a second victory, making his first political speech in June in a pleasant conversational tone and a frank style which, to Halley's delight, clearly showed sympathy with the working classes.

In the event, Pollock's largesse, and the loss to the electoral strength of many working men because they received parish relief during an influenza epidemic were among reasons for a drop in the Liberal vote though Halley retained his seat by 4,660 votes to 4,334. His majority was 326, compared with 747 in 1887. From the balcony of Westbourne House he publicly thanked Jane for her wifely support. He was to need her care more than ever all through the winter, for after the strain of the election he was gripped by a bronchial infection which did not finally leave him until April. As Spring returned, he wrote guardedly to a friend to say that his physician, Sir Andrew Clark, saw no reason why he should not live the ordinary span of life.

6. LAND FOR THE LABOURER

IN Parliament, the Liberals were settling down to another period in office with Gladstone, at eighty-three, Prime Minister for the fourth time. On April 6, 1893, the Grand Old Man moved the Second Reading of his new Home Rule Bill in the House, with Halley back in his seat and Jane in the Ladies' gallery. Eighty days later it was finally accepted, after many a battle in committee, by 301 votes to 267—only to be crushingly defeated by a packed House of Lords where a mere 41 supported it against 419. Halley shared to the full the sense of outrage caused by this reversal of the will of the Commons. Peers were bad enough, he thought, and parson peers were worse. He looked back a hundred years over the great Acts of Parliament designed to promote the welfare of the people and found the Bishops had opposed them nearly all. For Gladstone, whose conviction on so many points had become his own, Halley was truly grieved. When the old man's failing eyesight made retirement inevitable in March 1894, his last speech was on the subject of reform of the House of Lords. 'His retirement comes to me like a personal bereavement' wrote Halley to the *Spalding Guardian*. 'The loss is inexpressible. He might have been forgiven if he had lingered over his own past. But with Gladstone the cause is all in all, and his last words are a trumpet call to battle.'

The threats to Halley's health again grew menacing. Apart from the bitter disappointment of the Home Rule defeat, he deeply resented the fact that the eighty nights of toil, effort and pain they had devoted to it in the Commons—'part of our fast passing lives'—should be contemptuously written off by the peers. To help conserve his energies, he cut out the weekend travel to London by moving in August 1894 from Park Mansion, the St Leonard's property he had built for his family and for Jane's school, to The Firs, Clapham Park. Thereafter the collegiate school for girls at Park Mansion was taken over by Miss Agnes Booth, but the Stewarts retained ownership of the house. They were sufficiently in touch with St Leonard's for Spalding Liberals to have an excursion there and be entertained by the Stewarts after the 1895 General Election—a repetition of a similar day trip from Spalding in September 1888, when lunch was prepared for the party at Park Mansion.

How they must have loved the house and how unwillingly faced family upheaval in leaving it. One echo of their withdrawal from St Leonard's is preserved in an inscribed testimonial presented to Halley by the Sussex County Congregational Association and Home Missionary Society at their Autumn assembly. After fifteen years he had resigned the treasurership, and they acknowledged the 'deep interest, wise suggestiveness, business tact and generous aid' placed at their service. The Association hoped that 'in affairs Christian and philanthropic, national and municipal, the valuable services of Mr Stewart may continue to be exercised'. At the church where the family regularly worshipped together, the congregation presented an album with an appreciative address. Four miles from Westminster, the Clapham house, with four storeys and balustraded parapet, stood in four acres of ground, so the Stewarts were not hemmed in by bricks and mortar. Trees, lawns and winding drives hid stables, pigsties and cow sheds. Before long these were brought into use, cows, goats, pigs and poultry bringing farm life in miniature to the property and good home-made butter to the house, via the newly-equipped dairy. There was also a laundry, two women coming regularly to The Firs to do the washing. Halley fitted up a billiards room, added a second tennis court in the grounds, and went cycling with his sons in Clapham Park.[1]

When deep frost gripped the country in the winter of 1894-95, he and Jane escaped for a time to the romance and the sunshine of Italy. But congestion of the lungs again laid him low. His audiences noticed the change in his appearance, and privately he shrank from the strain of another general election. The issue had to be faced when Lord Rosebery, who had been leading the Liberal Government since Gladstone retired, decided in June 1895 to go to the country. The Party was divided between support for him and for Sir William Harcourt, his rival for leadership, and Halley, now aged fifty-seven, reluctantly agreed to stand again for Spalding in the absence of a younger candidate. This time Percy was election agent for the campaign as Richard Winfrey was himself standing for South West Norfolk, and for the second time Harry Pollock represented the Spalding Conservatives.

In the election address from Clapham, Halley claimed the Liberals had removed burdens from the tenant farmer, the occupying owner, and the labourer. 'To your interests I am doubly pledged: by the political convictions of a life time and by my business, which is absolutely dependent upon the prosperity of the agriculturist.' It was a miserable

[1] Halley retained ownership of The Firs until 1928 when he sold the house and grounds to Spurgeon's Orphanage at their figure of £5,750, the current market price being then put at £8,200.

election, with more interest taken in what the candidates said of one another than in their views on national problems. What Halley and Pollock said of one another's business acumen in the previous election was dragged out and dressed up, with Halley defending himself and Winfrey supporting him in the *Guardian* and Pollock serving writs for libel on them both. If Pollock meant to muzzle them, he certainly did not succeed, but the tactic may have helped towards his election by 4,623 votes to 4,274, a majority of 349. Pollock then withdrew his writs. In the country, the tide flowed against the Liberal Party and many of Halley's friends lost their seats. It was a moving experience for him and Jane to say Goodbye to Spalding and once more to be drawn by a friendly, cheering crowd to the station. Both of them spoke of their great disappointment, and of the even greater kindness that had made their association so warm all along. To assure them still further of that kindness, the Spalding Division Liberals in December presented them with a silver candelabra, and a silver tea and coffee service and tray, at a gathering in Halley's honour.

'I shall never pass an allotment or smallholding in England without being grateful that I was able to fight the battle of access to the soil and help you to live as Englishmen should.' The remark, made after his defeat, showed how deeply Halley felt the labourer's need. He and Winfrey could look back on very real progress in meeting this need, particularly so in 1894 when they and three local Liberals formed a syndicate to take over Willow Tree Farm, made available by Lord Carrington. They got possession at Lady Day 1895 and offered smallholdings on the farm to those who had already made a success of the smaller allotments. The syndicate shortly afterwards was enlarged and renamed the South Lincolnshire Small Holdings Association. It took over many more acres, overflowed into Norfolk, and by 1900 was known as the Lincolnshire and Norfolk Small Holdings Association. In the winter the smallholders meet for their annual supper and Halley, as president, was often in the chair. Lord Carrington himself was sometimes able to be a guest. For ten years Halley had spent himself in the cause of the underprivileged Fen folk. With their humble shillings they bought him a tray. He, on his part, offered land, and with it the right to be their own masters.

It is difficult for us today to imagine the admiration and gratitude that must have stirred the hearts of these men as they saw in Halley, in Winfrey and in their colleagues the genuine champions of their cause. They may have been inarticulate but they knew where to turn in trouble, as did Richard Skells, a Cowbit smallholder, in the Autumn of 1892 when faced with the closure of the mortgage on his house and land. At sixty-six he feared ruin and with only a week to go asked Halley, for whom he had three times voted, to loan him £800. He would send him the deeds and accept any rate of interest he was asked, because 'I think you would not undo me'. Halley sent the letter to Winfrey so that he could intervene quickly on the spot, and in a sympathetic letter to the old man wished it was in his power to meet his request but 'I have not £800 uninvested'. It would seem that, well off though he was, Halley disliked idle money as much as idle men, and made it work for him unceasingly.

There had already been one wedding in the family when Reginald Halley Stewart, the eldest son, was married in June 1893 to Mildred Stevens, a tall striking girl with black hair and fine grey eyes, daughter of Dr George Stevens of Newington Green. In June 1896, after a holiday in Cannes and Italy with Jane and their daughter Louise, Halley saw his second son, Percy, married to Cordelia, daughter of Sir Compton Rickett, Liberal M.P. for Scarborough. Both sons settled down to married life and as junior partners in the oil seed business shared in its operations at Rochester and in London, being joined in 1896 by their younger brother Bernard on coming down from Cambridge with an honours degree in Natural Science. Percy had the particular responsibility of supervising the fleet of barges taken over in 1895 from James Fox and Company, Thames Wharf, Limehouse, and used to transport the mill products and materials. With their red sails, on which the initials S.B.S. were boldly marked, the barges were one of the most familiar sights on the Medway. The Kent Oil Company was also taken over, and letter headings describe the firm of Stewart Brothers and Spencer as seed importers and crushers, oil refiners and oil-soap makers, importers of oil cakes, guano, etc. with a London office at 18 Bishopsgate E.C.

The enterprise was proving very profitable, and by now included plant to make soap—it carried the same trade mark, 'S.B.S. Pure', as the cattle cake—and to produce dyes from the colouring matter of the cotton seed oil. Ebenezer, who initiated these by-product experiments, employed a first-class chemist, but in time found a kindred spirit in his nephew Bernard who, with his knowledge of chemistry, strengthened the team in the refinery. Memories of brands of S.B.S. soap being tried out in Stewart households still linger.

Reception at The Red House for Research Fellows of the Sir Halley Stewart Trust, 25 September 1935

Research Fellows, *back row*: Dr A. F. N. Hughes, Dr G. D. Greville, Dr Van Rooyen, Dr J. L. D'Silva, Dr J. D. Day, Mr J. T. Phillips, F.R.C.S., Mr C. F. G. Ransome, Mr L. Goodman, Dr A. A. Levi, Mr A. T. K. Grant, Professor Noel Hall;

Middle row: Dr F. G. Spear, Dr W. Jacobson, Dr B. C. J. G. Knight, Mr F. Lloyd Warren, Dr B. Peters, Dr A. C. Frazer, Dr K. Madders, Dr H. Lowenthal, Dr A. M. C. MacPherson, Miss K. Milward Smith, Dr M. C. Scott Williamson, Dr D. J. Williams, Dr S. Nevin.

Trustees, *sitting*: Mr R. P. Winfrey (acting secretary), Dr Albert Peel, Mr Stanley Unwin, Dr Bernard H. Stewart, Sir Halley Stewart, Sir Percy Alden, Dr Sidney Berry, Mr H. B. Shepheard.

Not present: Mr P. Malcolm Stewart, Dr T. Hywel Hughes (Trustees); Dr E. R. Boland, Dr E. J. Conybeare, Dr Knott (Research Fellows).

Coat of arms granted in 1922 to Halley Stewart, then a 'Gentleman without title'

The motto had been his father Alexander's, engraved on his personal seal, a wax impression of which is seen in this picture

Halley had a small personal interest which had persisted from youth. As a junior clerk he had spent £200 on shares in a company prospecting for gold in Wales. Ebenezer invested another £200 and their father Alexander put in £100. The £500 came from Alexander's savings but it was all lost—though the Stewarts could boast of a pair of cuff-links made from the mines. Halley, however, never lost faith in the venture and kept in touch with developments. During his time in the Commons as a Member for Spalding the mines in Wales had yielded 50,000 tons of ore which produced gold worth £100,000. About four hundred miners were employed in the gold fields, half of them at Gwynfynydd. This mine was controlled by British Gold Fields Ltd, a company which had Halley as its chairman.

Though Halley had more time to give to business, he was often out speaking on Liberal platforms and was far from being a spent political force. The Spalding Liberal Association held him so close to their hearts that a final parting seemed unthinkable. They wasted no time in asking him to continue as their candidate but Halley could not accept. 'Spalding Division is a part of myself and to renounce it seems like maiming myself,' he wrote to Winfrey in January 1896. 'But I am quite clear that I have done what is right. A man without a history has made no mistakes, committed no blunders, alienated no sympathies. And a new man will put things in a new light.' Halley had just celebrated his fifty-eighth birthday when he declined this invitation. Jane, his always dear companion, was at sixty-two as great a comfort and a calm to him as ever, continuing to ease his path as much as she could by taking family problems and domestic cares upon herself. Their first grandchild,

Reginald's Gladys, was two years old. A brother joined her in 1897, the year that Percy's first child, Marguerite, was born.

He kept in touch with Richard Winfrey, who married early in 1897 (three years after his father's death) and settled in Peterborough, where he had obtained a controlling interest in the Peterborough Advertiser Company. The two men, sometimes with their wives, were guests in each other's homes, and on one of their visits to London in 1897 Halley was able to take Richard and Annie Lucy round the Copenhagen oil seed mill taken over at Limehouse. Just before Christmas that year all the London employees, ninety in all, were entertained by the company to dinner to celebrate the Limehouse development. 'The late proprietors were high-and-mighty Tories,' wrote Halley to Winfrey, 'and it was a new experience for the men to be talked to by a master who advocated trade unionism and the advantages of combination among the men, and the duty of voting according to their convictions'. He believed in the right to strike but also believed that after nineteen centuries of the Sermon on the Mount, strikes and lock-outs should not be necessary. There had been a lock-out at the Copenhagen mill before it was taken over and Percy, as its manager, secretly advanced money so that many of the men could redeem their suits from pawn to wear at the dinner. Limehouse homes were warmer that Christmas because the Stewarts, with their own individual type of christian—socialist—liberalism,[1] had come upon the scene.

[1] Keir Hardie, founder of the Independent Labour Party, first entered Parliament in 1892 but lost his seat, as Halley did, in 1895.

7. OUT OF MILLING

THE Stewarts were by now a wealthy family and a prosperous partnership. Halley, Ebenezer and Knowles Spencer had worked together in harmony long enough to reap enviable rewards from their enterprising team work. Indeed, their success seems to have been in advance of some other sections of the oil cake industry, where things were not going so well. Imports of oil seeds into the United Kingdom continued to rise in the nineties, depressing the price of oil cake, and farmers found it increasingly to their advantage to feed stock on cheap cake in spite of their own hard times. Uneconomic cake prices, combined with the activities of an American speculator seeking to corner the market in linseed, led to a number of bankruptcies. In and near Hull, which had for years previously been the natural home of the seed crushing industry because to it came the country's main seed imports from the Baltic ports, at least half a dozen firms broke. There was much talk among the milling fraternity of amalgamations to eliminate vicious competition and cut-throat pricing.

The Rochester partnership were alive to dangers and possibilities alike. They saw London replacing Hull as the natural destination of oil seeds as imports rose from other parts—Egypt, India, South America and the United States. They saw the country's livestock showing an increasing appetite for cattle cake. They saw mills, cursed by poor management, antiquated machinery or badly-selected sites, compelled to shut down—among them one at East Peckham, close to Branbridges and, in the same county, Wateringbury and Dover. Their own wisdom in producing high quality cake in a new mill, with adequate transportation on the doorstep, had been fully justified. Their business was sound and they had considerable assets. In the six years ending 1896 their turnover had been upwards of £2 million but bad debts had never amounted to more than one shilling per £100. While there were fears and failures among other companies, Stewart Brothers and Spencer considered the moment opportune for forging ahead. In 1896 they began active planning to form themselves into a limited company as Stewart Brothers and Spencer Ltd to attract additional capital, believing the time was ripe for opening a new mill in London. Their project was for a mill to be erected at Silvertown, where Prince Regent's Dock wharf with a frontage to the Thames of 240 feet was to be purchased. The whole site exceeded four acres, adjoining the Silvertown station of the Great Eastern Railway, from which there would be a private siding. Cost of site, buildings and machinery was put at £50,000, and an eventual crushing weight of 900 tons of seed per week was in mind.

A handwritten prospectus of October 16, 1896, shows the aim was to launch the new company with a capital of £100,000, the directors taking the whole issue (amounting to £60,000) of the preference and ordinary shares. The balance was to be offered in the form of £100 debentures at 4 per cent. 'Confident of the unrivalled facilities and advantages of this company, the directors,' it was stated, 'forego all charges and fees for their services as directors and managers until the debentures are paid off, looking for their sole remuneration to the results of their management in the deferred reward which will come to them in their dividends on the ordinary and preference shares.' Surviving in the form of printer's proofs, other suggested prospectuses were drawn up during the winter of 1896–97. Some retained the company title of Stewart Brothers and Spencer Ltd. One showed that the directors, with Halley named as chairman, were thinking of London Oil Seed Mills Ltd as the name; another was headed the Economic Oil Cake Mills Ltd. Capital for the new company was at one stage proposed at £240,000. The changes showed that considerable caution was being exercised, and the plunge into expansion was not immediately taken. Halley and his partners were feeling their way through a difficult situation. As they pondered the expansion of their own enterprise, a group of other millers were considering schemes to combine in order to form a stronger unit.

Meanwhile other influences began to work. As the months passed into 1898, John Richard Bartlett and his colleague Edward Flash came over from New York to try to amalgamate all British seed crushers into one corporation. However, they had omitted to prepare the ground properly beforehand. Negotiations failed through lack of proper contacts and they were obliged to retire temporarily from the field. In 1899, on their return to England, their position was more favourable, and they met nearly all the leading seed crushers, including Halley and the partners. As a result, a scheme of amalgamation was agreed t., with July 11th as the effective date. On that day the British Oil and Cake Mills Ltd came into being, still today operating with great success as part of the Unilever empire. Seventeen independent businesses co-operated in this far-sighted venture, responsible between them for twenty-eight mills. Of these, sixteen were at Hull and Gainsborough, three in Scotland, three in Liverpool, two in the West Country and three in London, with the Rochester undertaking completing the number and Halley having an acknowledged influence on the whole proceeding. BOCM Ltd was founded with an authorized capital of £2,250,000 and an initial issue of £1,750,000, comprising 550,000 4¼ per cent first mortgage debenture stock, 600,000 5½ per cent preference shares of £1, and 600,000 ordinary shares of £1.

Working from the Hotel Cecil, his London headquarters, Bartlett promoted the company and bought and re-sold the seventeen businesses to it at a profit for a total figure of £1,368,000 plus the value of stock-in-trade and movable plant. It was agreed that he should receive £700,000 in cash, £125,000 in debenture stock, £200,000 in preference shares, £200,000 in ordinary shares (making £1,225,000) and the balance in cash, debentures and shares as convenient to the board of directors of BOCM. The balance included Bartlett's remuneration and all expenses in setting up the company. The eleven original directors, with Hugh Colin Smith of Hay's Wharf as chairman, were all drawn from the existing mills, included Knowles Spencer,[1] and aimed to preserve the continuity and individuality of management of each of the amalgamated businesses. Heads of businesses forming BOCM Ltd agreed not to engage in oil seed crushing on their own account anywhere in Britain or abroad for the next ten years, and plans made by

---

[1] At some time subsequently, Knowles Spencer went into business on his own as a broker, dealing in oil seeds, seed oils, and oil cakes, and also acting as a trade arbitrator from his office at 2 New London Street, E.C.

Stewart Brothers and Spencer to forward their family enterprise went into cold storage. The partners were paid out in cash and shares, but the exact amount which the business realized is not known, though it is believed that Halley sold out close to his own figure. A copy survives of an estimate tendered by him showing the total value of various properties and allied items as approximately £350,000.

While schemes for expansion and/or amalgamation had been giving the partners such serious thoughts, Ebenezer became seriously ill in 1898. He was then sixty-five, Halley sixty-one, and Knowles Spencer fifty-six. It was an added reason for selling out for, on recovery, Ebenezer's doctor advised him to retire from business. He therefore arranged to leave Glendevon, his home in Strood Hill, Rochester, took a house at Westgate-on-Sea, and moved there to live in retirement. He and Halley and the rest could look back with pride on the success of their schemes, on the solid service they had provided for agriculture, and on the splendid lead they had given as employers of labour. They took farewell of their staff at a grand dinner on December 15, 1899, in the Castle Hall, Rochester. The menu shows the meal to have been substantial and the entertainment varied, and photographs of Halley, Ebenezer and Knowles, with Percy and Reginald, were reproduced on the ornate folder. This, no doubt, became a memento in many a Rochester home, and the family must have been glad that the big change in their own affairs was not to prejudice the fortunes of their labour force.[1]

Not long afterwards Halley himself received a

---

[1] The mills continued to operate as a vital part of BOCM—successfully so, in fact, until 1954, when they were closed down after serious flooding from the Medway.

memento—a clock which his fellow partners presented to mark their keen awareness of the vital part he had played after the fire in re-building, and later in realizing the value of, the business. It was Ebenezer who sought to put into words this sense of indebtedness, in a letter written in January 1900. 'One thing is certain,' he wrote, 'that this issue would never have been attained had it not been for the man at the helm —that man being yourself. To cap the whole, the successful part you played in the inauguration of the company which has taken over our business and properties, the negotiations which brought the scheme to maturity and the shrewd manipulation of the various points involved in the settlement (in which we all share)—all this compels our acknowledgment. We know the pressure and the anxieties which have characterized the past; we rejoice in your freedom from these today; we hope that freedom will be long enjoyed; we trust that you will be long spared not only to us but to all who love and honour you, and that in the joy which comes from service rendered to others your joy may be full.' In a postscript, Ebenezer added a tribute to Jane. 'She has been so closely intertwined in the ups and downs of S.B. and S. that it would be ungracious and peculiarly lacking on our part if we did not link her name with yours: the burden and the aid rendered has been hers as well as yours. Our thanks are due to her too; and as she and you are, in life and thought and experience, inseparable, I am sure I am right to add these words on behalf of the others as well as for myself.'

To Percy, who was then living at Blackheath, went the task of choosing the presentation clock. He was able to write to Ebenezer that same January to say he had bought it for £28 (plus £2 for a bracket to

support it in the hall at The Firs) at Vine and
Thompson's in Aldersgate Street. They themselves
were the makers of the clock, which they claimed
would go for 200 years and still have good working
parts inside its handsome mahogany case.

8. INTO BRICKS: IN AT GREENOCK

WHATEVER plans Halley had in mind for occupying himself without the oil mills we cannot say. Certainly, speaking must have been one of them for, of course, he had never given this up, and it was political campaigning which led to a surprising business venture and the creation of another fortune. Among Liberal platforms from which he discussed current topics had been one at Peterborough in 1898, soon after Richard Winfrey began to make his presence felt in that city. Here he rekindled the old fires at an Eastern Counties Liberal Federation rally, and was asked in May 1900 to become the Peterborough candidate. He did not accept at once, having already declined Grantham and Spalding. South Africa had replaced Home Rule as the dominant issue and had already led to further divisions in the Liberal Party. One effect of these had been the resignation as leader of Sir Henry Campbell-Bannerman. It was the year of Gladstone's death. Halley was among those who felt the Boer War could have been avoided and who had pleaded for sanity. He was with others who did so facing the crowds in Trafalgar Square before the outbreak of war in 1899, but jingoism gripped the people. They stormed the Nelson's Column platform and 'drove us away as if we were criminals'. 'Pro-Boer' was the taunt flung at such men, and war fever went so far that at Hastings a street named in Halley's honour was re-named.

His age, and divisions among the Liberals at Peterborough, made him hesitate over the candidature. There was some feeling that Mr A. C. Morton, defeated at the previous election, should be invited. Before the situation could crystallize, Lord Salisbury unexpectedly decided to go to the country in October 1900 on the issue of fresh support from the nation for the war. The campaign was quickly nick-named the Khaki Election, Morton accepted another constituency, and Halley agreed to oppose the sitting member, Sir Robert Purvis, an energetic barrister. Winfrey, contesting the South-West Norfolk seat, placed his house at Halley's disposal. But what could be done in ten short days? He drove round the division in a carriage and pair with Jane and their daughter, visited, spoke, and quickly became a popular figure. 'You might easily have got a man to serve you with fewer years and greater ability but a man truer to your cause—never. I am pledged by forty years of fidelity to be true to my principles, and I hope and believe that after me will come sons and grandsons to continue the work. What I learned from my own father's teaching I have in turn handed down to them,' was one of his striking comments as he wound up the campaign.

Even his opponent acknowledged that the impact he made was impressive, and the Tory majority was reduced by a third. A longer campaign might well have reversed it, but Halley lost the day by 160 votes. Elsewhere, Winfrey cut his opposition majority to sixty-six and Spalding made up for losing Halley by returning another Liberal, Mr H. R. Mansfield. The Tories were back in power, among their new Members being two future Prime Ministers, Bonar Law and Winston Churchill. Halley was again offered the candidacy immediately after the election. He believed Liberalism would triumph after the war and that Peterborough would share in it (as indeed it did) but that others—possibly his sons—would be carrying the standard, with his own life and career drawing to its end. So he did not accept.

While Halley had been waiting in 1900 in hope that divisions in the Peterborough Liberal Party would be healed before he agreed to become their candidate, he had taken the plunge back into business, and was now deeply involved in a new venture—bricks. Old Alexander Stewart would have seen in this opportunity yet another example of the Divine Providence of which he wrote so feelingly in his diary. Two of the leading Liberals who joined Richard Winfrey in urging Halley to be their candidate were the brothers George and Arthur Keeble. They had irons in several fires and business deals led them into diverse fields. From them Winfrey had acquired his interest in the *Peterborough Advertiser*. They experimented with a Norfolk process to produce fertiliser. They were also in the brick trade in Fletton, near Peterborough, and had the chance to acquire from Mr B. J. H. Forder of Luton his lime, cement and brick works.

The Keebles invited Halley to join them in financing the development. He agreed, supplying the greater part of the capital and becoming chairman of a new company, B. J. Forder and Company Ltd with a total capital of £280,000, which took over the business. The other directors were the two Keebles and Halley's son Percy, who took over the management. Percy had turned down the offer of a managerial post at £1,000 a year made by the new oil and cake company, preferring to keep with his father. With the Forder take-over went the unexpired portion of the lease of 'Wardown', the large house built in Luton in 1877 with grounds and lodge gate (now a public park) which Mr Forder had been renting for his own use from an Irish solicitor. Halley and Jane left Clapham in the summer of 1900 to make their home there—a move which Mrs Stewart welcomed as her health was affected by the London fogs. It was not long before Halley and the Keebles were in disagreement over financial policy. They wanted quick returns but could not budge their chairman from his views that profits must be ploughed back until reasonable reserves had accumulated. It might take ten years, they protested, but Halley insisted that even if it did, there was no other way to build a successful business. In fact it was fifteen or more years before Forders paid any dividend except on the preference shares. So the Keebles accepted Halley's offer to buy out their share of the business at a good profit.

Percy's brothers were not involved. After the sale of the oil mills, Reginald went to Canada for a time. On his return he took up management of a company of wholesale provision merchants called E. R. Stone & Co. Ltd, whose headquarters were at West Marina, St Leonard's, and in which Halley had acquired a controlling interest. In May 1906 Halley and Mr Lereculey of Brighton formed a company under the name of Stewart & Lereculey Ltd to carry on both the Stone and the Lereculey businesses, with Reginald as managing director and his father as chairman. It was a substantial undertaking with warehouses in a number of South Coast towns, among them St Leonard's, Brighton, Eastbourne and Southsea. Reginald also acquired a personal shareholding in the Brighton and Hove Supply Association Ltd which owned the Palmeira Stores. In June 1918 the name of the company was changed to Stewart Limited, under which title it continues to operate. As it happened, Halley was obliged to confess as time went on that he found bricks to be much more interesting than jam or tea![1]

Bernard had been in the mill against his real inclination. Passionately devoted to sport but denied many of its triumphs because of a cartilage operation on his right knee after a school football match, he joined Rochester Fire Brigade volunteers for fun and exercise and later became an officer. Turning out to a fire in the mill refinery where he worked and helping to save it was an unforgettable experience. When, relieved from business, he enrolled as a medical student at Guy's in 1899, the brigade presented him with a handsome snakewood stick with carved ivory handle and inscribed gold band.

Bertie Jane Louise, Halley's only daughter, for whom he always had a special affection, was thirty-one when she was married in 1902 to Ernest Cecil Haram, a stockbroker five years her senior. He had proposed to her when they were driving round Regent's Park in a hansom cab, and the wedding itself was in London, at the King's Weigh House Congregational Church in Duke Street, Grosvenor Square. Halley arranged the reception at the then fashionable Langham Hotel, the pair going off to Venice for the honeymoon. He and Jane gave them as wedding presents the canteen of silver and the Bechstein grandpiano which graced the home in Surbiton where they settled. The bride, with her brothers, had fluent French, for they had a French governess as children. Moreover, she had attended finishing schools in Germany and France, and had

[1] As a provision merchant, Halley was one of the first customers of the Danish Bacon Company Limited, formed in 1902. From early profits, DBC paid a bonus divided equally between factory staffs and customers, and Halley presided at a dinner given by English customers to DBC heads in honour of the first bonus paid.

thereafter been a great help to her mother in running the school at Park Mansion. Here, among other things, Halley would see to it that she was trained in money management. She never forgot the day when, as a young woman of eighteen, she learned he would make her a dress allowance of £20 per year. 'If you cannot manage on £20 a year I will reduce it,' he said, and when Louise asked if he really meant the reverse, he said 'No'.

The wedding year saw the end of the Boer War, and also an invitation to Halley from the Greenock Liberal Association to speak on Balfour's Education Bill. The Nonconformists were up in arms against this measure which, while expecting them to pay rates, gave them little say in the management of the schools. The Liberals found it a rallying cry in both Parliament and country, and Greenock warmed to Halley's fire as he treated the subject. And was he not himself a Scot? Though, as a Free Trader, Halley's views on sugar imports did not please Greenock's sugar refiners, he made such an impression in all other ways that by the end of the year he was looked upon as the next Liberal candidate. The selection was formalized in September 1903, at a time when Joseph Chamberlain's advocacy of Imperial Preference had become the big issue in British politics.

Halley did not yield at once. He told Winfrey in April that he had practically made up his mind to decline Greenock—'in many respects an ideal constituency. . . . I don't seem to know how to look at things from a mere party point of view. My hobby is to get down, down to the bottom of things, below party and creed, and to establish in the electors' minds some principle that will make them thinkers in the political sphere'. He knew his views were injurious to the sugar refiners and felt this inhibited his campaign. Yet 'I mean to fight once more. The taxes on the poor and the Education Act and now the London Education Bill have brought me out of my lair. I want a seat that is hard to win but not wholly impossible. I do not want a safe seat in Parliament, but I do want to capture a seat'. Greenock was not a safe seat. The sitting Member, James Reid, was a Tory and an old resident. Travelling to the constituency entailed long journeys. After his meeting there in September 1903 he caught a chill on the way home, and pleurisy and pneumonia laid him low for several weeks. Yet in January 1904 he was back in Greenock declaring of James Reid: 'I intend to shake the reed—to shake the Tory Member out of his seat.'

Halley indeed seemed possessed of a new aggressiveness since his recovery though he sometimes spoke of his sun as westering. He showed no weakness, either, at Luton where in February he refused to pay the rate under the Education Act, along with forty-five others in the town and thousands of other objectors throughout the country. In court, gravely and responsibly, being himself a magistrate, he urged objection to the law on behalf of them all. The Mayor, grieving deeply, did his duty and issued an order for payment against 'one of the best men in the town'. It was fascinating news for the hardy Scots of Greenock, many of whom respected Halley all the more for the stand he took. Early in 1905 David Lloyd George spoke there for him, regretting that he had thought fit to retire from the House when he did. Finally, in December of that year, Campbell-Bannerman was called to office by the King and at once went to the country. Halley and Jane started their electioneering on New Year's Eve—forty years after their first visit to Greenock on their honeymoon.

The recriminations which had marred work in the Spalding Division were forgotten in what was a happy campaign in Greenock, where Reid was a friendly opponent. Halley loved an argument and found hecklers fun. When one of them once asked what he meant by 'differentiation', Halley replied: 'If I am drunk and you are sober, there is a differentiation between us.' The heckler, somewhat befuddled, complained: 'Mr Chairman, the speaker accused me of being drunk.' Not at all, Sir,' retorted Halley. 'I accused you of being sober. Mr Chairman, I beg leave to withdraw the accusation.' In Greenock he advocated Free Trade, cheap food, and trade union rights. He opposed the Tories' Protection proposals. He promised to consult with the constituency on the local effect of the 1902 Brussels Sugar Convention.

Jane and Reginald were at his side for the eve-of-poll address when 5,000 people crowded the doors to listen to him. Voting was on January 18, 1906, Halley's sixty-eighth birthday, and Greenock celebrated by electing him their Member with 3,596 votes, a majority of 342. The Liberals were returned to power on the Free Trade issue in one of their greatest victories, with Campbell-Bannerman heading a team which included Asquith, Lloyd George and Churchill and enjoying a majority in the House (with Irish and Labour allies) of 350. In South-West Norfolk Winfrey shared in the general victory with a majority of 903. At last the two old friends were in Parliament together.

Halley meanwhile had had some house-hunting to do in view of the 'Wardown' lease expiry, and during 1904 had settled in the pleasant Hertfordshire town of Harpenden at The Red House, a substantial property standing in its own grounds on a hill above the town centre and close to the railway station. Here he and Jane spent the rest of their lives, enjoying visits from their children and grandchildren, entertaining guests in their own quiet way, thinking fruitful thoughts, and indulging generous impulses. From here Halley would emerge, as Member bound for the Commons, as company chairman with City appointments, as Nonconformist to assist a Congregational or other religious cause, as Christian citizen to champion a right or expose a wrong. Indeed, there was no small stir early in 1906 after his election when he went to meet a deputation of unemployed men marching from the Midlands to London. As they came through Harpenden, he strode at their head, and addressed them outside the town. 'I am an employer of more than a thousand men,' he said, 'but I am not such a fool as not to know that it is on them that I depend for what I am and have. Is it not true that labour should have something to say about the distribution of wealth it produces?'

It was revolutionary talk and the papers at Greenock and elsewhere spoke of it as such. But Halley did not hide his satisfaction at seeing Labour and Labour-minded Liberals becoming a force in Parliament, and one imagines that he relished contact with Keir Hardie and Arthur Henderson, those early Members, now joined by Ramsey MacDonald, Philip Snowden and J. R. Clynes. He loved being back in the House and though he spoke but little in debates, his faithfulness can be judged from his record of attendance—four hundred out of the five hundred divisions marking the first year of new Liberal rule.

Halley's indignation against the Lords raged with new fury when they wrecked the Liberal Education Bill of 1906. He felt that their day of reckoning would have to come. He was firmly persuaded, too, that education, the making of citizens, was a State affair, and that Christianizing of individuals should be left to the churches.

Halley had the great satisfaction in 1907 of seeing the Liberal Small Holdings Act safely on the statute book, a measure which owed much to Winfrey in his capacity as Parliamentary Private Secretary to Lord Carrington, who had taken over the Ministry of Agriculture. Twenty-two years had passed since they had toured the Spalding Fens together and started fighting for a square deal for the labourer. Now they had a Prime Minister who aimed 'to make the land which had been the pleasure ground of the rich the treasure ground of the people.' They had a huge majority in the House. They could point to the unrivalled success of their own Lincolnshire and Norfolk Small Holdings Association, and Winfrey in particular had all the details at his fingertips. For his part, Halley had undertaken a visit to Denmark to see at first hand the progress made there in setting up smallholdings. Winfrey, when guest of honour in April 1907 at a National Liberal Club dinner held to celebrate the passing of the Act, saw in it one of the fruits of the ties between him and Halley which had first been forged in the fires of 1885. In June 1907 both men were among the 8,000 guests invited by King Edward to a great garden party at Windsor Castle, comparable in splendour only to the gathering at Buckingham Palace which had marked Queen Victoria's Diamond Jubilee. The two friends moved among men and women of great distinction and it was Halley's pleasure to meet among them Mark Twain, the American author.

It was Halley's lot in September 1908 to visit Berlin as a delegate to the Conference of the Inter-Parliamentary Union on behalf of International Arbitration, which reflects his interest in the rule of law and reason between the nations of the world. With what eagerness, too, he welcomed the Old Age Pensions Bill piloted through the Commons that year by Lloyd George, who had become Chancellor of the Exchequer when Asquith succeeded Campbell-Bannerman as Prime Minister. 'Now, it only remains for them to introduce a scheme of insurance for sickness and unemployment,' he wrote. And the money must come not by taxing the poor but from the pockets of the wealthy. Halley had seen great advances towards the betterment of his fellows, but much land still remained to be possessed by the friends of progress and reform. At seventy-two he knew that the fires which burned within him in the cause of Liberalism were far from spent, but when Greenock Liberals, looking ahead to the next election, invited him to stand again, he declined on the ground of age. He foresaw the possibility that he might be returned to sit in Parliament until his eightieth year, and felt he should step down while he could still assist a younger man as his successor.

In the event, Halley's service as Member for Greenock ended more abruptly and much earlier than he had imagined. For in 1909 Lloyd George's 'People's Budget', which called for significant increases in taxation to pay for extra naval strength and for old age pensions, was fought by the Tories in day and night sittings which went on from April to the August recess and severely tried Halley's patience.

The struggle resumed and the Bill was not passed until November. Within a week the Lords had thrown it out. Asquith and his colleagues knew that the time had at last come when the nettle of Commons–Lords relationships had to be firmly grasped. He branded the action of the peers as a breach of the constitution and a usurpation of the rights of the Commons, and obtained the consent of King Edward to take the issue to the country. In January 1910, the country backed the budget in a General Election which saw the Liberals with their Labour and other allies back in the saddle again with a majority of 124, and Halley could congratulate Greenock on returning another Liberal, Godfrey Collins, as their Member. Later he was to accept from the constituency an illuminated address—one more for his store of souvenirs—as a mark of their 'respect, love and admiration'.

9. POTENTIAL PEER

IN July 1910, Lloyd George's new budget was accepted by the Lords, but meanwhile the death of the King in May delayed action on the Parliament Bill by which the Government determined to curb their powers. Edward had given Asquith an undertaking that, if necessary, sufficient peers would be created to carry the Bill in the Lords, and in November, George V endorsed this promise, contingent upon the country renewing support of the Government in a General Election. With the King's consent and without delay, Asquith once more submitted the Liberal programme to the electorate and the party was returned to power in December in virtually the same strength as before. How Halley must have missed the fever and the excitement of the momentous days which followed in the House. Lloyd George's schemes for health insurance and unemployment were passed, an allowance of £400 per Member was provided for, and in May the controversial Parliament Bill triumphed in the Commons. This robbed the Lords of any power over financial Bills or over any other Bills if passed three times by the Commons, and fixed the duration of Parliament at five years instead of seven.

So the year 1911 unfolded, with the full drama of the Parliament Bill still to come. Not till after the Coronation of George V did the storm break, when in July the Lords sent back the Bill to the Commons with their amendments. These Asquith refused to accept, and roused the Tories to passionate fury by disclosing that he had Royal support in dealing with certain eventualities that might arise. On July 24th he was shouted down in the Commons by the Opposition for a full hour before the Speaker adjourned the House. As he stood there, waiting to be heard above the unimaginable hubbub, he had in his possession the names of 249 prominent men of Liberal persuasion whom he would recommend to His Majesty for elevation to the peerage should this be necessary to ensure the adoption of the Bill by the Lords.

Late in the evening of August 10th, Lord Morley defined for the Lords the attitude of the King in words which George himself had approved earlier in the day: His Majesty would assent to the creation of 'peers sufficient in number to guard against any possible combination of the different parties in opposition by which the Parliament Bill might be exposed a second time to defeat'. Now gravely, now stormily, the Lords debated the extraordinary situation, a situation which found them pressed to sign their own death warrant. Many Tory peers sought to salve their consciences by abstaining, but before the lights went out in the chamber that night the House had decided not to insist on its amendments. The Bill was through—but only by the narrow margin of 131 votes to 114. The list of 249 potential peers survives in Asquith's papers. Among them are such household names as George Trevelyan, Bertrand Russell, Gilbert Murray, Thomas Hardy and J. M. Barrie. And there, too, is the name Halley Stewart.[1]

From time to time severe illnesses had punctuated Halley's career, and neither he nor his doctors had

---

[1] The list is printed without alteration as an appendix to the biography *Asquith* by Roy Jenkins, published in 1964. In *Leaves from My Life*, published in 1936, Sir Richard Winfrey recalls seeing Halley's name in the list some time after the event.

any reason to suppose he would outlive the normal span. On retiring from Parliament in 1910 he was seventy-two, and glad that no longer must he sit through endless talk in the House during the kind of all-night sitting that marked the Parliament Bill. However, his fund of energy showed no sign of becoming spent and Halley now had more time to give to business, to speaking, to Congregational activity, and to a number of other interests including affairs in Harpenden itself. When distance came between him and his friends and fellows, his powerful and winning gift of speech was transferred to paper. He moved men through his letters. He comforted them in times of distress with words that revealed the pastor's heart behind them. He challenged them in times of apathy. He clarified current issues in times of indecision. He elucidated problems in times of perplexity. He chided and praised. His letters glowed with life and warmth. They streamed incessantly from his desk in the study at The Red House, penned in the neat quick hand which never seemed to change. It is no surprise that so many of his family and friends could not bear to throw them away and that so much of his thinking is still preserved in this form.

Halley had no formal secretarial help, and Jane saw to it that nothing on the desk or in the study was disturbed, however untidy either of them might look. The room was on the ground floor of The Red House looking West to the hill rising on the far side of the town. Jane's boudoir was next to it. The study was, in fact, Halley's office, for he was far removed from the typical businessman who travels regularly to City premises to deal with colleagues and affairs. He worked from home, leaving management to executives on the spot but at no time relaxing his grip on financial policy. He visited offices and works for directors' meetings and consultations, being looked upon with awe by the staff. In the board room his word was law. Always punctual himself, he was irritated by late arrivals and did not hesitate to rebuke Percy or any other director for lateness. 'You must be here five minutes beforehand to compose yourself,' he would say. Between visits his letters, whether welcomed or not, conveyed his wishes and his advice. With so deep an insight and with so clear a facility for expression, it took courage in board room or in correspondence to question either his decisions or the arguments which led to them, and it was usually the higher wisdom to accept his leadership. But though Halley did not suffer fools gladly and was rarely at a loss for a quick and often devastating retort, he was never intentionally discourteous. If he disagreed with another point of view, it would not be before he had paused to lend a sympathetic ear to it.

The brick, lime and cement company of B. J. Forder and Son Ltd was developing in a gratifying way with Percy Malcolm controlling the works side as managing director and Halley advising him on the financial side. It was because Halley would not consider an investment giving less than eight per cent that preference shares in the brick company were fixed at this unusual rate. Making bricks—bricks to build houses, houses to provide homes—appealed to Halley's sense of service to his fellows. He had less interest in lime and cement. Perhaps he had slightly less confidence too, for one Harpenden anecdote is of Halley coming upon a workman using cement made by another manufacturer. 'Why are you not using Forder's cement?' he demanded. 'It's no good,' said the man. 'Well, I am Forder's, and I'm sorry you're not using my cement,' said Halley. But the man stood his ground. 'I don't care if you're Forder or not. The cement's no good and I'm not using it,' he insisted. Whether this unofficial piece of market research affected Halley or not we cannot say, but in 1912 this side of the business became part of the new British Portland Cement Manufacturers Ltd, which company Halley joined as a director. British Portland was a combination of most of the important cement-making firms which were not already part of the Associated Portland Cement Manufacturers Ltd, formed in 1900 by the amalgamation of twenty-four companies. Linked financially, APCM and BPCM produced most of the country's output of cement, of a quality which earned for it a world-wide reputation. Halley's connection with cement was a short one, but Percy carried it on till his death in 1951. The two companies developed into what is known as the Blue Circle Group under his outstanding leadership, and his name is inseparably associated with this great enterprise. It is another story, a second Stewart business romance—a record which shows how well Percy profited from his father's tutelage and how much of the Stewart genius he himself shared. For it was Percy who went on to make the name of Stewart at once the greatest name in bricks and the greatest name in cement, and in so doing helped to change the aspect of our cities and the face of our towns. He added fresh honours to an honoured name, and made a fortune greater than his father's.

Halley had lost two brothers, Philip and John, by death in 1908, and Kezia, co-founder with Jane of the school at Hastings, died in 1912. A much greater blow was the death in his eightieth year of Ebenezer on January 24, 1914. Though opposites in some ways, they had meant so much to each other all their lives that Halley felt truly bereft. Though he did not feel the pull of public life to the extent that his brother did, Ebenezer played his full part in city and church and was once invited to be Mayor of Rochester—an honour he declined as he could not give adequate time to the office. Before his retirement he had been a pillar of the city's Congregational church, was responsible for the Strood mission church until it could support a minister, and frequently spoke at religious, temperance and political gatherings. After giving up business he continued to work unceasingly for the Congregational cause. Every mill worker was known to him personally, and his warm humanity, livened by a sense of humour, won the regard of all. How could it be otherwise with one who shared so much the strength of character of his father Alexander and the lovable qualities of his mother . . . ?

Without the support of such an elder brother, Halley's story might well have been different. Philip and John were among the relatives who would come to Ebenezer for advice in financial and family difficulties. When resources were limited he would take their requests to Halley, whose inevitable response was 'I'll do whatever you do, Ebe.' The family had, indeed, early learned to stick together under Alexander's fatherly eye and Halley himself had been glad of this, notably when he lost a lawsuit in 1869 and John and others had set on foot a subscription for him.

Ebenezer's family had never seen so unhappy a man as Halley on the day he attended the funeral. 'I knew your father forty years before any of you were born,' he recalled as they drove with him to the station. And to Ebenezer's son Guthrie he wrote:

'I have lost the companion of my boyhood, my comrade who trudged with me to the City sixty years ago, my partner from 1870–1900. We were Brothers.' They were entirely united in their political views and in their loyalty to the Congregational cause. No one was more pleased than Ebenezer at Halley's political success, nor knew more surely how to trace the source of his convictions. Both of them continued throughout life the practice of family worship, and just before his last illness, Ebenezer took the unusual course of writing out the prayers he offered during the last two weeks of 1913—each of them full of gratitude and of longing still to be of service. The outlook of both brothers is faithfully echoed in Ebenezer's final petition: 'Help us to serve Thee by always striving to help our fellowmen. Awaken within us a sense of responsibility for everything Thou dost entrust to our care; help us to use it aright, so that we may at last render up unto Thee our account with joy and gladness and not with grief.'

Guthrie had entered the Rochester mill office in 1893 at the age of eighteen, and when Ebenezer retired and moved to the coast, he transferred to the London office of the company. Though, on leaving school, he had wanted to train at Sandhurst and make the Army his career, Guthrie did not serve in the Boer War but his younger brother Frank, who had studied at the Slade and in Paris, first made his name as a war artist at this time. Through Halley, he had been introduced to Sir William Ingram, proprietor of the *Illustrated London News*, in which most of his sketches of the South African war appeared.[1] On the formation of B. J. Forder and Son Ltd in 1900,

---

[1] After serving in the 1914–18 war, Frank became one of the leading hunting artists of the day.

Guthrie accepted from Halley the post of chief accountant, later becoming company secretary and, in fact, remaining as such with the brick company till his retirement in 1949—apart from service in France for which he volunteered in World War I. Halley once said of his nephew: 'Many men have valuable qualities, but Guthrie has qualities which are invaluable.' He and his sisters were among relatives who were invited from time to time to stay with their Uncle Halley and Aunt Jane, and they never forgot some of Halley's dining table repartee and its immediate effect in stimulating conversation—and laughter. One of many instances of this occurred when Guthrie found himself involved with Halley in discussion which threatened to go beyond dinner table limits. 'I think, Uncle,' he said, 'I had better not say any more or I might get out of my depth.' Like a lightning flash came Halley's quick retort: 'But Guthrie, I hear you are an excellent swimmer.' Guthrie's tactful withdrawal gave Halley the chance to have the last word, in which he always delighted. Many a political heckler must have rued the day he drew upon himself the rapier-like thrusts of a man with such a gift. But there were times when Halley did not realize its effect. When Bernard took his future wife to The Red House on an early occasion as his fiancee, she was left to spend a short time alone with Halley. Asked to sit down, and anxious to avoid any chair which might have been his own accustomed seat, she said, 'Which is your chair, Mr Stewart?' The sharp reply, 'They are *all* my chairs,' unrelieved by smile or twinkle, scarcely eased the strain of introduction for one so new to his ways.

Before another year was out, Europe was at war, fighting as Asquith put it, 'in defence of principles vital to civilization'. Halley supported him without reserve. At a party in 1915 at The Red House for a contingent of non-commissioned officers from the Lincolnshire Regiment, he declared to the men: 'Peace-loving though I am, my whole heart and soul tell me that this war is right. It had to come simply because the whole fabric of religion was in danger of being torn to shreds.' The party was the major celebration—apart from a remarkable family gathering—of the fiftieth anniversary of Halley's marriage to Jane. A splendid cake from his former constituents at Spalding was one of the most touching of the many gifts, showing again how strongly forged were the ties that still bound together the champion and his old friends. Meanwhile one of those old friends, Richard Winfrey, had been elected Mayor of Peterborough in the Autumn of 1913 and had received a Knighthood in the 1914 New Year Honours. The Lincolnshire and Norfolk Smallholders presented him with an illuminated address to mark the distinction.

After the golden wedding he invited Halley to visit Peterborough again, and Halley took this opportunity of once more seeing his Fenland supporters. Their outing included a call at the Willow Tree Farm holdings, where Halley presented prizes for the best stock and told the men: 'These smallholdings are the harvest of the bread cast upon the waters from 1884 to 1895, when I was your active servant in the division. I rejoice that the work done then has been so magnificently sustained in all its operations. Even so, it is not the end. It is only the beginning—we will yet see the country richer in smallholdings.' Instead of the quiet cup of tea with a few friends in Spalding which had been suggested, Halley went on to find himself amongst a crowd gathered in the YMCA lecture hall to congratulate him on his golden wedding. The surprise left him tongue-tied. 'In this division it has been said that I am guilty of making long speeches, but this is a time when the power of speech has vanished owing to your overwhelming tribute.' But not for long. Soon the words flowed again as he recalled that every foot of the Spalding division was dear to him—that here he had for ever emphasized those broad human rights which can be claimed for all mankind. 'Hold these principles, understand them, fight for them,' was his ringing challenge, at seventy-seven as forceful and as moving as ever it had been.

With a Coalition Government prosecuting the war, there were fewer opportunities for Halley to make political speeches. The war made inroads into his own affairs. He shares family anxiety over nephews away in the Forces, including Guthrie and his younger brother Frank; grieves with his brother George over the deaths of three grandsons; and laments the loss of his brother Josiah's only son Alec, killed in the Battle of the Somme and awarded the DCM posthumously in 1916. His youngest son Bernard serves in Army hospitals overseas: 'He has the reputation of being an expert surgeon.' (Bernard had, in fact, studied to some purpose once he was freed from the oil cake mills, qualifying B.CH, Cambridge in 1904, MA, MB in 1907, and MD in 1911.) He turns with renewed vigour to the needs of Congregationalism. He sees the brick works slowly running down. They were not restful days. Mr Forder had started working the clay deposits at Wootton Pillinge, not far from the Bedfordshire town of Ampthill, in 1898 and the Stewarts had steadily increased the capacity of the brickworks until the 1914–18 war halted their expansion. In 1910 the works produced 48 million bricks, a very considerable quantity for those days. Labourers on the farms and in the villages were attracted by the improved wages offered by the industry and local people nicknamed the two sections of the works Klondyke and Kimberley. These became almost derelict as the war went on, and reorganization and re-equipment on a large scale would be imperative if the company were to exploit the full potential of the deposits and meet the immense demand of post-war years.

Meanwhile Percy, during the last eighteen months of the war, devoted his particular abilities to furthering the national effort. Assigned by the Ministry of Munitions to the Government rolling mills at Southampton, he found an outlet for his desire to serve in directing production there at a vital stage. He and Halley had long consultations and exchanged lengthy letters on the future of Pillinge. Inadequate pre-war plant would have to be replaced. Living conditions in the tiny hamlet would have to be improved. Additional labour would have to be attracted from further afield. It was a time for visions and for venturings; for old faith to be practised in new ways; for personal ideals to shine against a general post-war background of broken dreams and shattered hopes.

10. IN TRUST

IN 1918, Halley foresaw the eventual end of the Liberal Party in the Coupon Election which swept Lloyd George back into power at the head of a Coalition of Liberals and Tories. The Independent Liberals won only twenty-eight seats. The Labour Party took fifty-nine. Implacably anti-Tory, Halley disapproved of the Coalition arrangement and, incidentally, of Sir Richard Winfrey's support of it, by which he was returned unopposed for South-West Norfolk. He correctly prophesied the disasters which were to follow. He felt they were bound to ensue with the Commons occupied by the 'wealthiest and least representative group in any Parliament since the Reform Bill of 1832.' With no Liberal to support at Harpenden he spoke for Jessie Hawkes, the unsuccessful Labour candidate. 'The country is facing a period of reconstruction immeasurable in its far-reaching effects,' he explained. 'The Labour Party is out for the security of employment of the discharged soldier and as such will receive my vote.'

A letter to Percy in February 1917 reveals some of Halley's aspirations for the brick works employees. Percy had said all along that they would have to build cottages with allotments so that the men would have homes and gardens near to their daily toil. Halley heard echoes in this of speeches he was making in Spalding thirty or so years earlier, and went on:

'The day of democracy is at hand. And in Church and State and in the industrial sphere we have to adapt ourselves to new conditions. Can we not evolve for the artisan some scheme of genuine co-partnership? Can we not supplant conflict by co-operation, sincere, frank, complete? It needs an humanitarian at the head. A man who can see the nobility that is latent in every individual and possessed by every class of society. As an incident in such a scheme of co-operation, cottages and allotments would be splendid but they are no substitute for it. The day of Labour has arrived . . . The political sphere is almost closed to me, but if I can do anything in my eightieth year in the small sphere of B. J. Forder and Son to win from the men the enthusiasm in their work which you and I have given to ours, I shall feel that the last days of life are not the least fruitful.'

These were the conceptions, beaten out fine by Halley and Percy on the anvil of their own hearts and minds, which led to the creation of a model village at Wootton Pillinge and to one of the early examples of profit-sharing in industry. But some years were to elapse before these dreams could be made real.

Halley was as keenly responsive as ever to current and continuing needs. He strongly supported the Society for the Liberation of Religion from State Patronage and Control, and also the Secular Education League, which protested against taxes paid by all being used to support any particular religion. Both these organizations found an enthusiastic president in Halley. He gave his backing to those who were organizing relief for children in the famine areas of war-stricken Europe. But perhaps closest to his heart was the cause that was most nearly on his doorstep—the cause of the underpaid Congregational ministers of Hertfordshire. Not only did Halley propose a scheme to raise the minimum annual stipend from £120 to £200 but he also gave time and energy and finance to help bring this about. Himself a child of the manse, he remembered conditions when his father's salary was £100. He remembered, too, when as a young father with three children his own stipend was £120.

Motoring round the county, the old man pleaded the cause from pulpit to pulpit during 1919, and by the New Year of 1920 had the joy of knowing that funds had accumulated to meet the new minimum, with sufficient in hand to make an extra grant in the first year of £20 to each minister. From this achievement Halley went on to revitalize the work of the Luton Road Mission, for which Harpenden Congregational Church was responsible. Believing that the centenary of the church could not be better observed than by new premises for this particular outreach, he gave £500 towards purchasing a site and promised to add twenty-five per cent to donations given towards the £1,800 needed for the building. The arrangement was typical of his method, for he preferred to provoke people to good works on their own part rather than mesmerize them into inactivity. The response was adequate enough for the foundation stone to be laid by Halley on November 4, 1921, and by March 1923 the new mission hall was in use and free of debt.

In his ninth decade, Harpenden's Grand Old Man thought much about the pleasant town where he had made his home. When the railway line had made its way northwards from St Pancras in 1865 it was little more than a village of less than five thousand souls. Its development as a residential area beyond the fringe of greater London was a natural consequence, and within a hundred years there were four times as many residents. Halley was asked to join the committee set up to consider the form of a memorial to local men who fell in World War I. He pleaded for something which would serve present and future generations as well as recall past sacrifices, and the decision to provide a nursing centre and clinic as well as to erect a simple granite cross on Church Green owed much to his urging. Halley himself wrote the inscription on a tablet in the Centre: 'To serve the living and honour the dead, this Nursing Centre was founded and, with the Memorial Cross, was dedicated on October 9, 1920 to the memory of the men of Harpenden who fell in the Great War. Their name liveth for evermore.' The Centre was completed and opened for use in December 1923.[1]

Thinking of ways to use his resources to help other people gave Halley endless scope for pleasurable scheming and active planning, affording an outlet for those fresh springs that ceaselessly surged within. Memories of the Spalding Division were never far from the surface and in October 1923 he established a small trust in memory of Richard Winfrey's parents, Mr and Mrs Richard Francis Winfrey, in whose home at Long Sutton he had found such warm-hearted support and friendship on his early visits. The trust directed that income from £200 2½ per cent India Government stock should be used each Christmas to assist the poor and needy associated with Long Sutton Congregational Church, of which these old and dear friends had been members and office-bearers for so long. Sir Richard Winfrey and his sister, Mrs Coupland, were the first trustees. Today this trust

[1] The Centre, at 40 Luton Road, now (1967) accommodates Harpenden's health visitors and district nurses. Some clinics are still held there, and among other town clinics are those based at The Red House in its modern capacity as a hospital.

comes for convenience under the general supervision of the trustees of the Sir Halley Stewart Trust.

Disposing of his great wealth in a responsible manner became an increasing preoccupation. Some acts of benevolence are fully documented, for by them Halley planned to perpetuate an ideal or reinforce a principle. But what of the countless gifts that have never been recorded, the now forgotten generosity that relieved private distress or silently supported a public cause? One newspaper, commenting on Halley's philanthropy, claimed he would have been a millionaire but for the fact that he incessantly gave his money away—at one time at the rate of £340 a week. In truth, the man stands revealed in his handling of the money that business brought him. Understand his attitude to wealth, and the key to his character comes to light. He said often enough that after work people had been well paid and employers had received an adequate return for their time and capital, any balance should be placed at the service of the whole community. For it was the community who created wealth. Speaking at St Albans in 1911 on land taxes at the time of Lloyd George's famous budgets, Halley quoted the specific case of land in Cornhill worth £3 million an acre with an income of £120,000 a year. 'It used to be worth £10 and its annual income was ten shillings! Who created the increment?' he challenged. 'Every footfall in Cornhill for hundreds of years has helped to create it. The increment belongs to the whole of the people and not to any individual. . . .' Such was the theme to which he returned so often, now mystifying, now enraging so many of the richer but lesser men of his day.

Money in itself is a dead thing. The wrongful

giving of it can corrupt the donor and harm the recipient. But money put to work can be a living thing, sparking off new life as it passes along. Money in the service of a glowing personality or a compelling principle can recreate the one and reinforce the other —a vehicle for energy and inspiration. Halley had wanted dividends from his money, and his business genius was rewarded by solid financial return. But there were other, greater dividends that fired his imagination, stretched his mind, burdened his prayers and exercised his faith. He who had served his God by giving himself so fully to the service of his fellows desired that his wealth should now stimulate others to continue that service. His 'challenge' gifts to the Congregational churches and other causes were never intended to settle old debts but to inspire bolder effort and greater daring. He had spent a lifetime seeking to apply Christian doctrine to everyday practice, to make religion relevant, to enlighten the people and to improve their lot, and he was determined that his money should be used to stimulate thought and activity towards the same ends. Conventional giving left him quite unsatisfied.

Halley had already asked his sons Reginald and Percy to join him in a private trust to administer the income from 6,250 £1 8-per-cent Brick Company preference shares to provide certain annuities. These were in favour of his brother Josiah (five years his junior) and his wife Fanny; of Mary Emily Auger, Jane's niece and much loved by them both; of staff of The Red House—Mary Goss Gammon, Mary Finding and William Cant, the coachman; of two ministers—the Rev L. E. Dowsett of Harpenden and the Rev J. J. Poynter of Harrow; and of the Herts Congregational Union, the Liberation Society, the

Colonial Missionary Society and the London Missionary Society.

In 1924 he invited several distinguished Congregationalists to join Reginald, Percy and their younger brother Bernard as co-trustees with him in an enlarged trust which Halley endowed with a further 13,750 Brick Company £1 shares and whose objects he was at pains to clarify. Those who joined the family as trustees were Dr Sidney Berry, secretary of the Congregational Union, Dr Thomas Hywel Hughes, principal of a theological college in Edinburgh, Dr Albert Peel, editor of the Congregational Quarterly, and Mr Harold Beaumont Shepheard, of Shepheards, Walters and Bingley, Kensington solicitors. The first charge laid upon them in the Trust deed signed by Halley on December 15, 1924, was to pay £1,000 annually for five years to the Herts Congregational Union, provided that in each year the Union themselves raised £3,000. If they raised less, the Trust would contribute proportionately less. Halley wished the income so raised to provide a capital fund for church expansion within the county, for he clearly foresaw the movement of population and the need for new buildings.

He planned to transfer the bulk of his securities to the Trust, whose general objects are abbreviated as follows:—

1. To advance religion.
2. To advance education.
4. To promote charitable purposes beneficial to the community, in particular: a. to assist to discover means to apply 'the mind of Christ' to extend the Kingdom of God by preventing and removing human misery; b. to study Our Lord's life

and teaching in their application to social relationships; c. to express the mind of Christ in the realization of the Kingdom of God upon earth and in a national and world-wide brotherhood; d. to arrange lectures and sponsor writings aimed at attaining the objects of the Trust; e. to support research in social, economic, psychological, medical, surgical or educational subjects exclusively connected with the objects of the Trust.

Further provisions dealt with grants to libraries, publications, societies and persons furthering the same causes. Halley determined that the Trust should not identify itself with any particular sect or dogma other than what he described as the 'cult of the science of God as manifest in man, in the Son of Man in the person and teaching of Our Lord.' He also provided that two members of the Halley Stewart family should be among the trustees, and that any new trustee should certify in writing his full sympathy with the objects of the Trust. If the Trust could no longer call upon any two members of the Halley Stewart family as trustees, the Finance Committee of the Congregational Union of England and Wales was to share in the task of appointing new trustees.

From his private fortune, Halley transferred further large sums from time to time to the Trust and these were formally listed in a schedule to a further deed dated October 21, 1923. They included shares in British Oil and Cake Mills Ltd, British Portland Cement Manufacturers Ltd, and London Brick Company and Forders Ltd. More than 67,000 shares in the latter were transferred, giving the Trust a holding at that date in excess of 87,000 £1 shares.

11. A HOUSE MOURNS ITS MISTRESS

THE change of name of the Brick Company as noted in the Trust deed reflects its growing fortunes. It had been incorporated in 1900 as B. J. Forder & Son Ltd, with a total capital of £280,000, and with Halley chairman and Percy managing director. In 1923 it absorbed the London Brick Company and was known as London Brick Company and Forders Ltd. At that time the capital of the company stood at £750,000.[1] Soon after the amalgamation in 1923, executives of the company realized that the firm's title was an inconvenient mouthful and it was then shortened to London Brick Company Ltd, as it still remains, though the Forder side represented the bulk of the capital. Other smaller firms which had joined LBC included the New Peterborough Brick Company, the Star Brick Company (Whittlesey) and the Saxon Brick Company (Dogsthorpe, Peterborough).

It was in February 1924 that Halley, soon after his eighty-sixth birthday, having been chairman of the Brick Company for twenty-four years, decided to resign the office in favour of his son. The 1923 amalgamation had crystallized a wish to retire that had been in Halley's mind at least since 1920, when he had broached the subject to Percy. Anticipating the new chairmanship, he had then commented: 'If at any time any complication should arise in which you would like the opinion of an interested outsider, while my brain remains clear it will always be at your

[1] The figure for capital had risen to nearly £2½ million before Halley's death in 1937. In 1960 it was put at £8 million, and in 1966 was given as £17 million.

command.' His formal letter of resignation, now framed and in the possession of Percy's son, Sir Ronald Stewart, says of Percy that: 'From the first he has been managing director of the company, and to his wisdom and untiring devotion its development and prosperity are mainly due. I place on record also my great obligation to all who have been my colleagues on the Board and to the officers of the company for the valued assistance they have given me which has made the tenure of the chair an easy task and a constant pleasure.'

Halley was appointed senior deputy chairman and remained so till his death. He did not look upon it as a sinecure and was as ready as ever with advice, his letters to the new chairman being frequent and often full of complicated financial detail with hand-written balance sheets attached. Figuring these out in his mind would sometimes keep Halley awake at night. 'At last I was compelled to turn up the gas and put it down on paper. That done, I finally got to sleep,' was how he would explain it. Hearing that Percy would be unable to attend one of the Board meetings because of illness and that another director was to conduct the business of the day, Halley determined that a Stewart should be in the chair and saw to it that he himself was present to preside at the meeting in the company's Africa House headquarters in Kingsway, London.

In the summer of the year Halley vacated the company chair, he received a most interesting gift from his children which has now become a family heirloom—a large album of pictures forming a biography without words. Alexander is there, his hardships are recalled, his family and schools and chapels are pictured, followed by the many associations— business, political, religious and domestic—that crowded on to the canvas of Halley's own career. His children presented it to him on June 20, 1924 (his fifty-ninth wedding anniversary) as 'a token of affection and appreciation, and as a record of a courageous and inspiring life'. It was Bernard who, with the support of Percy and Louise, initiated this activity and spent many months collecting and identifying the material for the album, which forms a pictorial commentary to much of this present volume.

One glimpse into Halley's way of handling the finances is seen in a comment made to a friend in a letter of 1934 about the company's splendid profits. 'We are extremely conservative in our published figures. But the time comes when we can no longer tuck away profits as 'repairs and renewals'. I take no responsibility. I simply charge everything that has a possible resemblance to Repairs and Renewals to that account, and leave the office to fight it out with (i) our own auditors and (ii) the Inspector of Taxes. I place the responsibility on auditors and Inspector, and of course accept their decision even when in my judgment I think they are wrong.'

Among his colleagues on the Board was Arthur Thomas Worboys of Luton, who had joined Forders in his teens in 1900 as an office boy. In 1917 he had proved himself sufficiently to be elected to the Board and ten years later had become a managing director. He was one of the few brick company executives who paid personal visits to The Red House at Harpenden to discuss business matters. It is not surprising that Halley and Percy should from time to time feel the strain of the so-long-extended father and son relationship, and Worboys sometimes found himself charged with the delicate task of helping them to see eye to eye. On Halley's death in 1937, Arthur

Worboys became deputy chairman, and succeeded Percy Malcolm as chairman in 1950. He received a knighthood in the 1966 New Year Honours and died in November the same year, when Percy's son, Sir Ronald Stewart, took the seat after being for some years a deputy. Sir Arthur never lost his deep sense of respect for the first founder of the company, whom he had known for thirty-seven years. For shrewdness, he said, he had never met his like. On Halley's character as a businessman, he described him as just but not generous, making keen but fair bargains; a man who would never take advantage of anybody.

Just as in March 1937 Percy had paid tribute to Halley, his predecessor in the chair, so thirty years later history repeated itself. Sir Ronald, speaking in May 1967 at the annual company meeting in the Connaught Rooms—as his father had done before him—spoke of Sir Arthur as having become, despite a retiring nature, the leading authority on the affairs of the brick industry. Sir Ronald went on to recall: 'His outstanding financial and administrative ability came into prominence in the late twenties and early thirties when, working closely with my father, Sir P. Malcolm Stewart, he assisted in achieving the series of mergers in the Fletton (Peterborough) industry which formed the company as we know it today.'

Halley's nephew Guthrie, secretary of B. J. Forder and Son, became first secretary of the company with Mr Peter Fergusson, secretary of the London Brick Company, after the amalgamation of the two undertakings. Two other relatives who were given positions during Halley's chairmanship were at the Wootton Pillinge brick works. Members of the Auger family, which for generations was prominent in the oyster industry at Burnham-on-Crouch, now the

Essex yachting centre, they were among the seven children of John Auger senior, of Lambourne Hall (across the river from Burnham). His wife Marie was sister to Halley's wife Jane and the children would sometimes visit Harpenden, one of them, Mary Emily (born 1870), being Halley's favourite niece. He would hear from Marie and John Auger of the oysters which had made the family prosperous and prominent for two hundred years—and not only the Augers but the Richmond, Bygrave, Rogers and Hawkins families as well, as memorial windows competing for position in Burnham church would indicate. He would hear, too, of the oyster areas in the river which had to be cultivated; the hand-made dredges dragged along the river bed by sailing smacks and the oyster-sorting which followed; the depletion of the crop by over-fishing, by the multiplying of the slipper limpet and by the attacks of the American tingle—two of the oyster's deadly foes. Trade was greatly reduced, fortunes dwindled, and though John Auger as the eldest son remained in the oyster business, two of his brothers were glad to turn to bricks. William Alfred Auger went back to Burnham on retirement and Hugh Joseph Charles Pickering Auger settled and remained in Bedford.

With the Trust deed safely signed in December 1924, Halley must have looked forward to Christmas with more than usual satisfaction. But these feelings were chilled by Jane's illness, and on Boxing Day she who had given him unmeasured affection and unstinted care for nearly sixty years entered herself into rest. They loved and cherished each the other till death came to part them and their mutual respect and forbearance made a wonderful study in graciousness. One of Halley's comments, that she was 'clay in the hands of the potter', reveals what marvellous tact and wisdom she must have possessed, and confirms her affectionate carefulness in seeing that his wishes were observed in everything.

Though endowed with gifts of leadership and initiative Jane, in the manner of the time, had kept these completely in the background where her husband was concerned. But she was a woman of strong character, and had been accustomed as principal of her school to take the lead in everything and to speak to considerable audiences. Both her school and her large family had been managed firmly, lovingly and competently. As a scholar, Jane was specially at home in the French language, and also delighted in astronomy. Her boudoir at The Red House, next to Halley's study on the same floor, later became her bedroom. Towards the end of her life she would enjoy the loveliness of the gardens from a wheeled chair, but earlier she and Halley would often walk round them together. At family gatherings, as hostess to visitors distinguished or otherwise, or as welcoming townsfolk to charity garden parties in the grounds, Jane made her own gracious contribution and her children loved her deeply. Memories of The Red House are incomplete without her, and to family and staff alike she was always a sweet person to whom they would turn sometimes with relief after confronting the always busier, brusquer and more forbidding Halley.

Halley had taken the house at Harpenden when the lease of 'Wardown', their Luton home, expired in 1904. It had been built in 1892 by Vaughan Stevens, a London businessman who selected the site at Harpenden so that he could move from Chiswick. With his family and horses came William Cant the coachman, to occupy one half of the imposing lodge adjoining the stables. Four years later, on August 27th, the house was burned to the ground on the day before the Stevens family were due back from a holiday at Hastings. A fault in the electrical system run from a private generator was the suspected cause. This tragedy may explain why the house was lit by gas almost to the end of Halley's time there.[1] Stevens rebuilt the house on the same site to about the same size but in much plainer style, and its sale in 1904 was dictated by business reverses. A photograph of the staff he employed shows three gardeners, a coachman, cowman, cook, scullery maid, parlourmaid, housemaid, washer woman and two other assistants who were gardeners' wives. The family also had the help of a governess and a nurse.

When Halley first looked over the house, he was glad to hear about Cant and to agree to continue to employ him. 'My man at Luton has run away with the housemaid,' he told Mr Stevens, and Cant worked at 'Wardown' until the Stewarts moved to Harpenden, where they were the last family to keep carriage and pair. Cant was a familiar figure in white breeches and high silk hat, taking Jane for drives, meeting visitors at the station, or helping Halley with appointments. One of the horses was commandeered in the Great War, and this was the period when Jane went out in the Victoria which Halley then acquired. Best remembered of the carriage horses were Halley's handsome chestnuts 'May' and 'June', which were a source of pride in the town. Going out in the Victoria or the

[1] At eighty, thinking himself too old to change, Halley decided against installing electricity. At ninety, he agreed to it. Bertie Jane Louise (his daughter, Mrs Haram) arrived for a stay at the house just in time to prevent him arranging for only one light fitting in the middle of each of the large bedrooms.

brougham was, indeed, one of Jane's greatest pleasures, but there were times when Halley would interfere with these recreations by taking Cant, and sometimes the carriage as well, to London or Greenock or some other centre for prolonged Parliamentary visits, Cant attending him not only as coachman but as manservant. Theirs was typical of so many Victorian master-and-man relationships. On the one hand was demand, its weight scarcely eased by strictly measured generosity. On the other hand was loyalty, its strength permitting no ill word against the one served. When Cant allowed himself one day to grumble that he was paid only a boy's wage, Halley's retort—'Yes, and doing only a boy's work'—seemed natural for the one to make and the other to accept.

When drives were not possible, Halley's wishes were that his wife should walk in the garden for exercise, and he measured the paths so that he knew what was half a mile and what made up other distances. Jane's favourite walk took her to where the violets peeped. Halley's was longer, and skirted what was called the long field. Both walks became a tradition. Halley never cared for cars and never owned one, unlike Percy, who had a passion for driving. When he took a Bentley made to his own specification to Harpenden, Halley commented afterwards: 'I didn't care for his latest motor—it was a stinking affair.' Perhaps it was Halley's old love of cycling, a practice he continued to enjoy until in his seventies, which made him resent the appearance of cars on the roads before World War I. 'The fast driving of these machines in public places,' he said in a comment reminiscent of his Hastings complaint about horse carriages, 'is becoming a nuisance.

Since the invention of this snort-raising piece of ironmongery a new hazard to life has become recognizable'.

When Cant could no longer work after an operation in 1927, Halley would arrange to be driven out in a car hired from Putterill's garage in Harpenden. Mr C. F. Putterill recalls that he and Halley often discussed a standing arrangement for a car and driver to be available to him at any time, but could never agree on terms for this specialized service. A track which bounded The Red House property was made up and named St George's Way by the local council, after the large red brick school further along Carlton Road. When Halley demurred at this, the new roadway was re-named Stewart Road and is still so called, though the wide modern entrance to The Red House now opens out of Carlton Road.

It was Cant who persuaded Annie Mary Finding, a former housemaid with the Stewart family, to return to The Red House, and the two stayed on in service to the Stewarts for the rest of their lives. As Jane aged, with deafness and a faltering memory weakening her capacity, Finding became more and more indispensable in the house, and Halley gladly invited her to take over housekeeping responsibilities on his wife's death and to control the rest of the small staff. Her brother Joseph was for thirty-six years an under-gardener and on Halley's death, brother and sister lived at 3 Tennyson Road, which Halley had bought for Mary's use in retirement. She watched over the ageing Halley with a zeal which led some to call her a dragon, but this was only because she guarded his comfort with a sometimes over-anxious solicitude. She became a real companion, someone at hand to talk to or to be with for walks or drives. When

Halley attended services or functions, or went to Board meetings at the Africa House head office of the London Brick Company, Finding would be there to see he came to no harm.

He had had to overcome her housemaidly diffidence in decision, and a story which has long been a family classic illustrates this. Each morning Mary would go to Halley's room to ask what he would like for dinner. He would ask what she suggested, and invariably said: 'That will do very nicely, Finding.' In time he proposed that she should instead go into the dining room and ask the table what it would like for dinner. The table would reply: 'What do you suggest?' and on hearing her answer, the table would say: 'That will do very nicely, Finding.'

On a day later on, when Halley was well into his nineties, the dear soul was much distressed to see him go through the garden with ladder and saw. She followed hurriedly, to find him studying the medlar tree which no one else was ever allowed to touch. 'This branch must be taken off—and you know, Finding, I always prune this tree myself.' 'No Sir, really you must not attempt it. You are not fit to go up a ladder,' she pleaded. Reluctantly Halley gave way, but not without a threat. 'Well, Finding, if I don't take it off this year I shall have to do it next year—or the next after that. . . .!'

Cant died in 1934, Mary Finding in 1948. Miss Elsie Cant, the coachman's daughter, lives in retirement in Harpenden after a lifetime of teaching in Hertfordshire schools, and looks back nostalgically to the palmy days of The Red House, to the comings and goings of families and friends, and to the hours she played with younger Stewarts—grandchildren, nieces and nephews—on their visits.

Family prayers were a ritual at The Red House continued from the early days of Halley's married life. Staff, family and visitors were all included, and Jane had always regularly supervised the preparation of the room for this purpose at breakfast time, extra chairs being brought in. Halley's reverence for the Bible and his faith in God ensured that this religious exercise was never perfunctory nor formal but warm and living in its simplicity. 'To hear him pray was like listening to the spirit of a little child,' was how Dr Sidney Berry once described it.

12. HALLEY AT HOME

THE Red House became a refuge for Percy in 1906 when the health of his wife Cordelia gave rise to serious concern. He rented a house in Tennyson Road for the children and their nurse, and he and Mrs Stewart occupied part of the roomy accommodation in the stable lodge. Mrs Stewart died in September that year, aged thirty-four, leaving three young children and the memory of just ten wonderful years of marriage. With her fair golden hair, delicate complexion and sweet, shy smile she was indeed a lovely person and all who knew her grieved deeply at the loss. During her sad decline, much sympathy was shown by Beatrice Maud, a daughter of Joseph Bishop Pratt, distinguished as a mezzotint engraver, whose home was on the opposite side of the road, and in the spring of 1907 she and Percy were married.

Relationships between Halley and his children, grandchildren and nieces and nephews were not uniformly marked by the warmth and understanding that clothe so many childhood memories with delight. They looked up with awe to the commanding, bearded figure with his correct speech and often severe manner. He was strict with his sons, Reginald, Percy and Bernard, who inevitably felt overshadowed by their father's own high standard of achievement. Looking over the years it can be seen that the business interests which the two elder sons took up gave them a standing in Halley's eyes which Bernard, who was by nature no businessman, never seemed to share. His feelings of inadequacy deepened into a lifelong sense of inferiority and although, out of the oil mill, he began to find fulfilment and success in medicine, the relationship with Halley remained uneasy.

Bernard must have found his personal diffidence a handicap in discussion with his father, who was never accustomed to concede an argument easily. A hint of the atmosphere between them survives in the memory of the conversation they had about the telephone. Bernard, as a student, scientifically explained to his father that a voice heard on the telephone was not the voice itself but a reproduction of it. The exchange ended with Halley saying: 'Well, Bernard, I would rather think as I think and be wrong, than think as you think, and be right.' In undertaking to arrange the purchase of a partnership in a medical practice for Bernard, Halley seems to have looked upon the outlay partly as an investment and possibly, too, as a business challenge to his son, for the arrangement involved payment of five per cent on the purchase figure. Bernard was unaware of this at the time and it was a shock to him to learn the details. But he was meticulous in making repayment a first charge on his income, his wife Mabel supporting him by strict economies in their first home at East Bergholt, where they lived almost within a stone's throw of Constable's Flatford Mill. For four years they did not have a family holiday, and Bernard had passed his fiftieth birthday before capital and interest were cleared.

It was common for him to take time from his own busy practice to go over to Harpenden when Halley or anyone in the family or household needed attention. There were times when he personally delivered bottles of medicine, and though this freely-given professional service must have appealed to Halley's deeply ingrained business sense, it pleased him much to have his son's attention, and his confidence in

Bernard's skill and judgment grew steadily over the years. Indeed, as Halley went on further and further into old age, Bernard was among those who felt that, of all that was remarkable about his father, not least was the noticeable softening of some of his attitudes. Mabel always went to Harpenden when these visits were paid, and a bond of affection and trust developed between her and Halley. She took it as a great compliment when he commissioned her to buy all the kitchen equipment and curtains for the research centre opened by the Trust in Hampstead (more fully described in the next chapter), and she felt that his expressions of satisfaction were reward indeed.

In boyhood, the three brothers learned the wisdom of sending their sister Louise to see Halley if there was some childish request to present. Louise, the only daughter, was the object of so much of the sunshine in her father's reserved Scots nature. Their relationship was indeed a happy one, and in due time Louise's own daughter, Joan Haram, shared the same special affection with her brother Stewart. On their visits to The Red House Joan, perched on Halley's knee, would say to him: 'Grandpa, talk Parliament,' and Halley would obey! How his zest and vitality impressed her! How he laughed and wept over the children's little plays acted on the balcony at the end of the hall! How he loved the pianola—and insisted when Louise and the children left at the end of their holidays on playing 'Will ye no come back again!' And with what joy Joan would hail the day when they caught the Harpenden train from London for another stay.

Mispronunciations heard at table always meant that Webster's dictionary had to be consulted. But even Halley could not cure Finding of saying 'Burningham' instead of Birmingham and when he gave Finding a batch of shares in the London Brick Company for a Christmas present, he complained that she seemed more pleased to have the peppermints that were a gift from Joan's mother!

Jane in her lace cap can be remembered by the family quietly moving round the house, every now and then peeping into the study to see if Halley has all he needs. They will be together on Saturday mornings for the ritual of going through the household accounts, for there must be neither waste nor overspending. Needs must be real before they are met. The sons, on a visit, can say it's time a worn carpet is replaced—but Halley prefers to be seen next day on hands and knees with an ink bottle, dabbing in the bare patches. His daughter Louise posts a parcel which costs more than he expects. 'Then why did you not remove some of the wrapping paper?' he asks. He has a paper knife for opening all his letters, and uses it to cut off all blank portions of paper to be saved for further use. Of an afternoon or evening he is round the billiards table with a guest, quick stepping and competent with a cue, or out on the bowls lawn—but neither of them on a Sunday, and his skill at both hampered by his own impetuosity.

Yet strangely enough he will cut a hedge on the Sabbath, calming the querulous by saying: 'When the Lord stops the hedge growing on a Sunday, I'll stop cutting it on a Sunday.' To some who admire his flowers, his lawns, his greenhouses and the general loveliness of the grounds Halley quips: 'God Almighty and I made this garden but you should have seen it before I took it over!' If not the hedge, perhaps it is the vines that are being thinned, for Halley has immense pride in his black and white grapes and no one must touch them—nor the peaches on the wall-trained trees—but he. The strawberries, too, are almost as sacred, for they are not to be picked until the wedding anniversary on June 20th each year. For the big golden wedding day in 1915 twelve children were there, each one handing to their grandparents a golden spoon, the boys bowing to Jane and the girls curtseying to Halley.

Fare was simple at The Red House, for apart from a hatred of waste and extravagance, Halley had a type of nervous indigestion which compelled caution in eating. There was ham on the sideboard for breakfast, and Halley invariably had salt with his porridge. He was very fond of cheese, soup and fish, took very little meat, and usually drank a small glass of whisky and water with his evening meal. To clear soup he would add sherry, giving this treatment surreptitiously with a chuckle to some of his teetotal friends. He was never a teetotaller himself and met the tastes of his friends in this respect, even down to the small crate of beer provided for George Newton, Sir Richard Winfrey's chauffeur, when they drove down for a few days' stay. Few retorts to hecklers ever gave him so much fun afterwards as his assurance to a political and teetotal audience that he had been a 'non-smoker and a non-abstainer all his life'. For smoking he had little patience. Only in the billiards room was the habit allowed, otherwise family and friends had to go grumbling into the garden to indulge.

Visitors staying at The Red House found Halley punctual to the minute for breakfast at half-past eight, having had (until he was well over seventy-five) an early cold bath. For prayers which he regularly conducted in the breakfast room the maids joined the family, each carrying in her chair from the kitchen. At eleven o'clock, coffee was served; at one o'clock lunch. From a quarter-to-two to half-past, Jane rested, coming down dressed for a drive as the clock chimed the half hour. If she was not enjoying the pleasant Hertfordshire countryside, it would probably be St Albans that attracted her. She was back precisely at quarter-to-four, with tea at quarter-past. Billiards often occupied Halley until dinner at half-past seven, for which everybody changed. After coffee, the men mostly played billiards, and Jane always went to bed at ten o'clock. Frequently for Halley a fresh period of desk work now began in the study, words and figures keeping him busy as stillness settled over the whole house. Unless he had been out during the day he would himself have had a short afternoon rest.

Only on special occasions in the summer would Halley forsake his usual black coat and striped trousers with spats for a grey suit. Before age slowed his pace, he walked very fast. On Sundays, for instance, he would ask those in the house if they were going to church and all would say 'Yes', only to find that they had to start without him. Halley, catching them up and passing them before the church was reached, would get in first, and it pleased him to suggest the others had started earlier than they needed, and that he had found time for one or two more letters before he followed them. It was another simple pleasure to him to be in his seat before the others arrived, so that when they came in he stood up for them to pass along the pew. Halley's reading would seem to have been among the biographers rather than the novelists, though the crusading spirit that Dickens showed in some of his work cannot have been overlooked. He had a love of poetry, and from Tennyson would quote with approval the idealistic prophecies of universal culture and a new brotherhood of man. He found an echo of his own philosophy in James Russell Lowell's *The Vision of Sir Launfal*, where the prelude speaks of the beggar taxed for a corner to die in and heaven alone as given away. 'June may be had by the poorest comer—And what is so rare as a day in June? . . .' How often, midst summer delights, Halley would quote the question, and in so doing lift the thoughts of others to a higher level of appreciation. This must have been in his rarer moments of relaxation, for to those about him Halley seemed so often to be restless and preoccupied. It was something of a drama getting him away to catch a train or to attend a meeting. While Jane would invariably be ready in good time, Halley, though never late, would appear in the hall only in the last few minutes, watch in hand and impatient for the carriage.

Sometimes Joan would write simple verses and send them to her grandfather who, not to be outdone, fell to versifying in reply. In eighteen lines crowded on the back of a postcard sent to Joan at 'Wardown', home of the Harams at Woking, he wrote a piece of simple rhyming philosophy by way of encouraging her output. Here are some of them:

> You say that if you had the time
> More stories you would tell in rhyme.
> But if the time you will but seize
> For writing stories such as these,
> Twelve hours you'll find in every day
> In which you can your rhymes array . . .
> So please do send us a few more

Of tales of which you have a score.
'Corked luggage' if you duly think
Is useless when men want a drink.
So draw the cork, that nectar clear
May sparkle forth your friends to cheer.
For rhymes like these, your very own,
Delight us all, my darling Joan.

Joan's first bicycle was a gift from Halley, after he had seen her trying to ride one when she was nine. He himself had made great use of a bicycle and family rides had been a habit when time could be found for them. Halley may, indeed, have taken his bicycle on Continental holidays. A letter from him to Joan shows that he never forgave the attendants at the Monte Carlo Casino for not allowing him inside to look round because he was wearing knickerbockers. He made a point of entering St Peter's in the same clothes when he reached Rome, and chuckled many a time over the fact that the church welcomed the worshipper which the gaming house ejected! It was Halley who first introduced Joan to Continental travel in 1922 when, at the age of eighty-four, he took her and her mother to Montreux.

Once the legal formalities setting up his Trust had been completed, Halley did not waste time before seeing that it began to function. A month after the deed had been signed, he called the trustees to their first meeting on January 14, 1925, at the Memorial Hall in Farringdon Street, headquarters of the Congregational Union, and was appointed chairman. His first words were a wish that at all their meetings the trustees would have the conscious presence and guidance of Almighty God, whose Kingdom the Trust was founded to serve. Reginald Stewart was appointed secretary and treasurer, and the Trust authorized its first grant—£150 to the Hertfordshire Congregational Union extension fund as allowed for in the deed. The trustees met five times in 1926 and then approximately once a quarter. At the second meeting the question arose of lectures under the auspices of the Trust, and it was agreed to invite Sir Oliver Lodge, the physicist, to give a series of lectures on the objects of the Trust. Sir Oliver was living at Harpenden, had a friendly relationship with Halley and was well aware of his ideals. In October 1926 he started giving a series of six lectures under the general title 'Science and Human Progress', for which a fee of £600 was paid, including publication rights.

It was an outstanding occasion for Halley, now in his eighty-ninth year, and at the end of the first lecture he moved a vote of thanks to the Lord Mayor for presiding and for the use of the Egyptian Hall. In a glowing letter next day to Louise he recalled the excitement. 'Was not the gathering a great send-off for the first lecture of the first lectureship of the H.S. Trust? I am so glad that Joan and you, Percy and Beatrice, Bernard,[1] Mabel and Harold were there. When she is ninety, Joan will recall her visit to the Mansion House 'seventy-one years ago' as I recall going to business—the bank—on October 16, 1853, seventy-three years ago. How little I thought then that there would be a H.S. Trust meeting at the Mansion House with the Lord Mayor in the chair in 1926. I am glad to have lived to see the day and to drive down in state to the Mansion House in the splendour of my rich daughter's motor car. . . .' Halley expressed the appreciation of the trustees to Sir Oliver Lodge at the close of the last lecture when,

[1] Mabel and Harold: Bernard's wife and elder son.

as at the first, the hall could not accommodate all who sought to attend. A list of the distinguished speakers who lectured for the Trust appears at the end of this volume. Lectures continued to be arranged annually until the 1939-45 World War, but a regular pattern was never re-established following this interruption.

Those who lectured over the years knew they would have no more attentive listener than Halley. Some of them sparked off letters of agreement or disagreement from him, and a point put by Wickham Steed in 1933 made an old chord vibrate and sound as clearly and as strongly as it did in Halley's earliest days as a Liberal campaigner. In a letter on November 28th he wrote:

'I await with interest the full text of the Wickham Steed lecture to see how he justifies his argument that in any given enterprise the wage earners have a right to what he—Steed—deems excessive profit. I think I could make out a better case for the consumer. True, no labour would often mean no profit; but no consumer-buyer would always mean no profit. Undue profit in any factory, after liberal provision for unskilled labour has been made, belongs to the community at large, not to the lucky individuals selected by the factory proprietors. And if there are any who have the biggest right to share in the excessive profits or to absorb them wholly, in my opinion the workless denied access to the land to earn their own living, arising from our unjust land system, stand first. Surplus, excessive profits should belong to the State to serve primarily the have-nots and the little-haves, not first the lucky ones who have full-time employment and an adequate income as the fruit of their labour. My Trust is the cash expression of this conviction.'

13. THE TRUST AT WORK

Halley's eldest son Reginald, treasurer and acting secretary of The Halley Stewart Trust Fund and perhaps the member of the family who shared most fully his father's ideals for it, died on April 22, 1926. Besides Halley, relatives who had had a stake in his South Coast provision merchants business were his wife Mildred, his brothers Percy and Bernard, his sister Louise, and his cousin Grace, daughter of Ebenezer. Reginald's death at fifty-eight was bereavement indeed for family and trustees alike. The Stewart family sold their interest in the business, and no immediate steps were taken to fill the vacant offices in the Trust. At their meeting on May 20, 1926, the trustees agreed that a donation of one hundred guineas should be made to the National Playing Fields Association 'in remembrance of the late Mr Reginald Halley Stewart'. By this practical gesture they honoured both the man and also the eager interest he had consistently taken in the activities of this healthy movement.

Mr Stanley Unwin, the publisher (now, as Sir Stanley Unwin, himself chairman of the Trust) joined the trustees in the Summer of 1926 at the invitation of its founder. Halley had felt drawn to Unwin at a meeting held in 1923 to hand over the Pastors Retiring Fund to the Congregational Union. The original trust allowed provision for 'Independents' who were not necessarily accredited Congregational ministers, but the new scheme would not. Halley and Unwin were the only ones to speak against this (rightly, as it proved), and it was characteristic of the older man to warm to the independent spirit of the other.[1] He was then eighty-five and Unwin a mere thirty-nine—the oldest and youngest of those present—but as Halley's acquaintance with Unwin developed, he felt he was one upon whom he could depend to further the ideals of the Trust. Unwin's firm produced the lectures by Sir Oliver Lodge in book form, and became publishers to the Trust. The mutual affection and respect between Halley and Unwin deepened, and the latter had some difficulty, when Halley assumed the new office of president of the Trust in 1933, in countering Halley's eagerness to propose him as chairman at that stage. Both knew what it was to be immersed in public affairs, in business matters, and in church commitments, and both experienced setbacks from serious illnesses.

It was part of Halley's service to his family and friends to cheer them with letters, and in these his faith and philosophy easily broke surface. It was natural for him to commiserate with Unwin over his neuritis and to say: 'What a mystery is undeserved suffering! "HE suffered" thus. The disciple is not above his Master. . . .' Always it seemed that Halley could link detail with vision, practice with faith. When Unwin sent him information about Miss Margaret McMillan's pioneer children's nursery in the East End, he wrote in reply that he had been exhilarated by an imaginary visit to it. 'The Deptford shadows were all eclipsed and I said: "So many glorious things are here, noble and right." ' And then follow characteristic quick-fire questions. 'You want to raise money for another shelter. How much? From whom? Whose property will it be when erected? Is

[1] See Sir Stanley Unwin's autobiography, *The Truth about a Publisher*, 1960, page 202.

THE RED HOUSE,
HARPENDEN, HERTS.

19 Dec. 1934

My dear Mr. Unwin.

I am greatly distressed to learn of your illness and hasten to write that come what may, I hope you will not dream of attempting to attend the meeting on Monday. I cannot on this it be possible for you to work your way here from the journey here & from the fatigue of the meeting.

I shall miss you very much. We all shall. But I need hardly assure you of my sympathy. If meeting comes to the same when we are not present. I am greatly tempted to cancel the meeting. I would do so if I thought it would be fair to those who have made arrangements to come.

With sincere hopes and wishes that the X-Ray may ease your doubts and his opinion, and that you will not rest content to do what is fit of daughters wife and self, I am,

Yours cordially,
Stanley Unwin

Solicitude at ninety-six

there in your mind any thought that the Trust can help? If so, how? There is no reference to finance in Miss M's letter. Has there not been an audited account?' Within a week Halley heard that Mary McMillan was admitted, partly paralyzed, to a nursing home. 'Is there anything to be done for her personally?' he at once asks. 'The Trust was not founded to do slum work, or to sustain slum workers. But it was founded to inspire and assist idealists to think, speak, write and act so that the nation shall be drawn or driven into slum abolition.'

How often the trustees were to hear Halley explain: 'The Trust was not founded to do this, or that.' Applications for grants came in thick and fast. Some were quickly met; others were partly met or put off pending investigation; many were declined forthwith. Interpreting the terms of his Trust and educating his colleagues into his own attitudes was a major task for Halley up to his death. Seeking to continue his work in the spirit in which he started it has since been a major problem for the trustees. In 1937 Halley, in a letter to Dr Peel, wrote that he was glad to have lived long enough to lay down the lines on which he intended the Trust to run. 'I have every reason to think it would not so well have fulfilled the object for which it was founded without the guidance of the founder for the first year or two. Every trustee has one or more good causes at heart, and the temptation would have been great to win for them the Trust's income. But the precedents of the first ten years are really the Trust's decalogue, and I am very happy about its future administration.' The letter was dated May 6th. 'Long may you be spared to influence its wise administration,' ended Halley. 'If I am spared until January I shall enter my 100th year. That's growing up!'

Dr Peel was, in fact, spared until November 1949, when his fellow trustees mourned one whom they described as an erudite colleague, known both for his historical and religious work. One letter from Halley in July 1923, which Dr Peel considered so typical of him that a copy should be preserved in the Trust archives, took the worthy divine to task for his 'culpable neglect' of the fourth commandment. 'The day stands for nothing. But the principle of the commandment is all in all and is not less mandatory for a parson's Monday than for his Sunday. I make your Monday a 16-hour day of work, and if rest is an obligation, how do you discharge your debt? Seriously, do discover, somewhere in the wild, some place and time for Sabbath keeping.'

Halley's passion for first principles was applied not only in personal life but in church affairs, for he goes on in this letter to comment on the Congregational Union's Commission on the Teaching of the Christian Church in regard to War, of which Dr Peel was chairman. 'Why of the Christian Church?' asks Halley. 'Why not go to the fountain head, the Church's Lord and Master? Why not "the teaching and mind of Christ"? Even the words of the Word do not express the mind of Christ. They are only the outward and visible forms, when received with accuracy, of the mind of Christ, which the living Spirit is ever unfolding in the life of Man, the Son of Man. Why bend the knee to the altar lit with church candles, when the light of the world is shining, lighting every man?' Halley chided Dr Peel on the fact that the Commission was clerical. 'It is an insult to our principles to constitute a Commission like that' he said flatly, and explained: 'To be clerically-minded is death—to freedom—whether the clericism be Papal, Salvation

Army or Congregational. To be congregationally-minded is life and liberty.'

Comments on the Trust made by Halley in letters and in conversation, and statements at trustees' meetings, have been treasured as revealing his outlook and desires. As early as 1925 he emphasized that he could have helped existing institutions by endowing them. But far wider was his dream. Ever changing conditions of life obscured the causes of social injustice and created new ones. But the living Spirit, ever near to guide successive generations, inspired new minds to grapple with old wrongs and reach out to new and diviner ideals. But, he went on, 'chill penury represses the noble rage of fertile minds and stifles their redemptive and creative aspirations.' He hoped his Trust would help bring freedom to those in bondage such as this.

Gradually the pattern emerged—help for the prevention of suffering rather than its relief; support for experiments, for research; assistance to individual pioneers rather than to organizations; elasticity in decision and a refusal to allow a dead hand to control the living. 'Every step we take is sure, sooner or later, to be hurled at us as a precedent,' he said in a letter dated June 1934. 'Now frankly, any grant we make to any one for any object is at our sole discretion, and gives to no one any claim whatever on the Trust. I am emphatic about this. The grant made to Westminster Hospital may be cited as a precedent. But I do not regard my first essays in grant-making, or any essay, as giving any one a claim on the Trust. And, personally, I am not bound by any grant as a precedent. So instead of repeating Westminster, I have profited by it and not done the like again.' Indeed, so eager was Halley to avoid setting precedents that he would often help a 'doubtful' case from his own resources rather than agree to the Trust doing so.

The financial policy which had built up his businesses and his fortunes was also applied to the Trust's funds. Annual income was never fully applied, and by careful handling the value of the investments steadily increased, so ensuring their extending effectiveness. In 1926 the gross income of the Trust was £10,500. In 1928, Halley transferred further securities worth £20,000 to the Trust to cover total payments of £10,000 for Congregational Church Extension in London, Essex, Kent and Surrey, at the rate of £2,000 per annum for five years, contingent on the Congregational County Unions themselves raising a further £1,500 each year. Failing this, the grant would be adjusted pro rata to the actual sum raised. It was the challenge gift he preferred to all others.

Later in 1928 a further £24,000 stock was transferred, and at times valuable shares in the London Brick Company offered at par were taken up, some to be realized later to the great advantage of the funds. The Trust, in fact, drew off five-sixths of its chairman's fortune, but he continued to supervise the holdings in the old masterly way, buying and selling as his knowledge and insight led him. From a figure in the earlier days of £200,000 the funds of the Trust increased in time to £350,000. The list of investments as they stood in 1933 appears as a schedule to a supplementary deed of October 21st. Halley regularly reported to the trustees on the value of the holdings and their expected income, so that they knew within what limits they could operate in making grants. In January 1935 the investments at current market prices, with the value of Trust property at Hampstead, were estimated to be worth as much as £412,000, yielding an income of £19,000.[1]

The property at Hampstead was the Halley Stewart Trust Physics Research Laboratory, made available to King's College, University of London, for research in the physical sciences—particularly for Professor Appleton's study of the electrical properties of the upper atmosphere—and opened in 1933 by Lord Rutherford. The premises, 30 Chesterford Gardens, had been bought and equipped by the trustees in 1931 as an institute for research into disseminated sclerosis and for the reception of patients suffering from it, but the project had to be abandoned when difficulties arose between the trustees and the research staff involved. Hospital, household and nursing equipment from the institute were stored at The Red House, for use when Halley's plan for its conversion into a hospital would materialize. King's honoured Halley in 1936 by electing him a Fellow of the College.

Being a trustee was certainly no sinecure. There were many applications to consider, many enquiries to be made, many difficult decisions to take, many deserving cases to disappoint. If Trust meetings were not held at its London offices, Halley would preside over them at The Red House, alive to every detail involved. For trustees who could stay, he would carve at dinner, keep them up talking as long as they were willing, and meet them for breakfast at half-past eight next morning. Memorable gifts from the Trust fund included £1,500 in 1929 to Lord Cecil's League of Nations Union disarmament campaign, and

[1] In 1968, for the first time, the income of the Trust in one year was expected to reach £50,000, with the market value of investments, property and land estimated at a little more than £1 million.

£5,000 in 1934 towards the £30,000 needed to save the agricultural research station at Rothamsted, close to Harpenden, and its land from the builder. Local children have reason to remember Halley because of the Halley Stewart Harpenden Scholarships founded in 1927 to provide three bursaries of £20 per year for Harpenden pupils, particularly those who failed to obtain the normal scholarships. From the time of the 1945 Education Act, these bursaries have helped Harpenden students with their expenses at colleges and universities. Halley arranged that appointments to fill vacancies among the local trustees should be made by the Halley Stewart Trust.

Few benefactions were so rewarding, however, as the help given to research students in hospitals and laboratories up and down the country. Here indeed was investment in human life and Halley lived to see splendid returns from it. The story would fill another volume, at which the official minutes of the Trust can only hint. Details of medical research work reported to their meetings were sometimes difficult for the laymen among the trustees to grasp, and they were glad to have the guidance of Dr Bernard Stewart, himself a figure in the world of medicine, and to call upon the advice of the Medical Research Council and other authorities.[1] Halley was not always content to leave others to make enquiries and recommendations,

---

[1] In his personal reminiscences published in 1945, Dr Bernard Stewart, who was president of the Trust for twenty-one years after his father's death, largely attributed to this the fact that he became a member of the Delegacy of King's College, London, and a Governor of Guy's, St Bartholomew's, Brompton and Harpenden Hospitals. In 1938 Edinburgh had conferred on him Fellowship of the Royal Society (F.R.S.E.). Among other later interests was membership of the Asthma Research Council and of Bart's Cancer Research Committee.

but himself kept in touch by letter and occasional visit with those who sought the Trust's help. As an instance can be quoted this letter of October 1932 sent to the trustees between meetings, Halley recalling that, 'having mentioned to the trustees at our last meeting, with their warm approval, that as the student research scholarships offered to Charing Cross Hospital were exactly the primary object for which the Trust was founded and that I wished them increased in number, I ventured to tell Sir Walter Fletcher (Medical Research Council) that on certain conditions to be agreed, I would propose to the trustees that a somewhat similar offer should be made for Queen Square Hospital scholarships. These research studentship annuities fully realize one of my chief aims in establishing the Trust. These command talent for research from post-graduate students which otherwise would be lost to humanity, because of the bread-and-butter needs of would-be devotees; therefore I do not hesitate to ask you to sanction my telling Sir Walter Fletcher that he may communicate these views to the members of his council.'

One of the most satisfying events in the life of Halley and in the history of the Trust was the unique reception at The Red House on September 25, 1935, when the trustees and research students were able to meet each other with the aged benefactor as their host. A photograph taken in the grounds that day shows him seated among his thirty-one guests—seven representing the Trust and the others being research fellows from such famous hospitals as the Brompton, Charing Cross, Ham Green (Bristol), King's College, London, Middlesex, National, St Bartholomew's and St Mary's. Several came from the Asthma Research Council and from the Strangeways

Laboratory (Cambridge), and the group was comcompleted by men and women from Edinburgh University, the Pioneer Health Centre (Peckham) and University College, all having established themselves in their respective fields. Three of their fellow grantees could not attend, and the two trustees absent were Percy Malcolm, the vice-president, and Dr Hywel Hughes, who was finding his age and the distance from his theological college at Edinburgh a bar to full involvement in the activities of the Trust.

Dr Sidney Berry wrote glowingly of the brief time he and his fellow trustees spent with these trained and skilled investigators who were dealing with problems connected with cancer, tuberculosis, diabetes, disseminated sclerosis, asthma and the like. 'This country has shamefully poor provision for those who want to use their knowledge and gift for research work, and most of those young men and women who are being supported by the Halley Stewart Trust would have been unable to follow their sense of vocation without the Trust's help. I shall not easily forget the vivid impression of the hour we spent together. These researchers will certainly make their mark on medical science in future years. Some of them may later on be famous for the discoveries they may make for the benefit of humanity. In the midst of such a company one could not help feeling the enormous power of generosity wisely directed. That informal meeting was a picture of the sacrament of giving.'

The research fellows asked Dr M. C. Scott Williamson of the Pioneer Health Centre at Peckham to thank Halley and the Trust on their behalf. He said the personal acquaintance made with the founder that day would be a great stimulus to their endeavours. Certain it is that none of them were likely to forget

Halley's response, moving in spirit and wonderful in phrasing, in which he stressed not the gift he had made to them, but the gift they had made to him. Never more clearly was the vision which created the Trust seen being realized before the eyes of its founder and of the colleagues who shared in its administration. Researchers were to meet each other again from time to time, and the Trust encouraged them to visit each other in their laboratories, meeting their expenses, but this first reception at The Red House stands out as a red letter day in the story of the Trust.

14. KNIGHT BACHELOR

ATTENDING with the trustees on the day of the first reception at The Red House was Richard Pattinson (Pat) Winfrey, their secretary and barrister son of Halley's old friend Sir Richard Winfrey. His acceptance of office in October 1928 ended an unsettled period which followed the death of Reginald Halley Stewart a year after the founding of the Trust. A new secretary had been found in Alfred Howe but ill-health cut short his services in January 1927. Three ladies were approached during the year with a view to obtaining their assistance, but no arrangement could be made. One of them was Halley's niece Grace, daughter of his brother Ebenezer and sister to Guthrie, joint secretary to the London Brick Company. Ebe's family had followed the development of the Trust with great interest, remembering that their father and Halley had so many views in common regarding life and work and wealth. 'We feel,' wrote Grace in a letter in 1966, 'that our father lived again (to quote Matthew Arnold) in the founding of the Trust by his brother Halley.' It was indeed a remarkable fulfilment of those shared aims and aspirations which had led to their first partnership a half-century earlier. Much as she appreciated her uncle's invitation, Miss Stewart did not feel in 1927 that she could accept. She was already involved with the Froebel Educational Institute College at Roehampton as secretary and remained so until giving up secretarial work in 1933. Halley well knew the service she had given to good causes, going back to her activities before World War I with the Young People's

Department of the Congregational Union, and during the war in the appeal department of the Serbian Relief Fund. In 1918 she was appointed secretary of the children's branch of this fund and organized support for it from Sunday Schools in various denominations.

Halley was glad, therefore, to have the help for a time of Mr H. A. Avis of Brighton, who had been secretary of Reginald's provision firm and had resigned the position after his death and the subsequent sale of the business by the Stewart family. Many a weekend saw him at Harpenden, for he dealt with Trust accounts, assisted in some of the Trust affairs, and attended to Halley's personal interests and private business arrangements, which were considerable. At that time Mr Avis was in his early seventies, an admirable person, friendly and capable. He not only bridged the gap in the Trust secretariat but made a good companion for Halley, sharing with him many an hour's enjoyment on the bowls lawn. Among his hobbies was the interesting one of repairing clocks and watches. He also helped Halley to keep in touch with his old haunts at Hastings and St Leonard's, where Park Mansion, the house he had built for his large family and Jane's school, remained his property throughout life. In 1930, although it was thirty-six years since he had left the town for Clapham, Halley presented a large silver cup for the Hastings Lawn Tennis Hard Courts championship, to be held by the Corporation with a miniature for the winner.

The final settlement of the problem of the secretaryship meant that fresh links between the Stewart and the Winfrey families were forged in the Trust. R. P. Winfrey, who in the early days of his service to the Trust saw Halley nearly every weekend, had read Law and had become a barrister (Middle Temple) soon after coming down from Cambridge. In 1924 he was invited to stand as Liberal candidate in the Holland-with-Boston by-election (in the old Spalding Division with Boston added). Then only twenty-two, it was Halley who encouraged him to forget the diffidence of youth and to plunge into the fight. Moreover, forgetting his own eighty-six years. Halley actively took up cudgels on his behalf and on July 24th spoke for a full hour at a thrilling election meeting at Boston, adding to an all-round review of the political scene a powerful appeal to the same principles which had brought him into the area forty years earlier. For a similar meeting in Spalding, the Corn Exchange was thronged beyond capacity by those anxious to see and hear the old hero. But despite Halley's dramatic intervention, the Liberals were denied victory at the polls.

Years later, on the death in 1946 of Dr Hywel Hughes, Mr Winfrey himself became a trustee, and is still actively involved in its affairs as treasurer. The London offices of the East Midland Allied Press Group of newspapers which he built up (including the *Spalding Guardian*, Sir Richard Winfrey's first acquisition) also house the office of the Trust and share the services of Miss Barbara Clapham, who became secretary in 1946. In Spalding, to commemorate the vivid days when Halley was Member for the Division, an open space was presented to the town by the Trust as a playing field. Fenced, planted and graced with entrance gates bearing the coats of arms of Spalding and of the Stewart family, the field was formally opened in May 1954 by Professor Harold C. Stewart, son of Dr Bernard Stewart, who by then was Halley's only surviving son but unable to be present in person. A parallel town improvement was the laying of Winfrey Avenue as a new road along a boundary of the field, named after Sir Richard and R. P. Winfrey. Thus for ever the association between the two families, which Professor Stewart recalled at the ceremony, is visibly perpetuated in the town where it began.

But this was not the only Fenland fruit to ripen years afterwards from roots which struck in Halley's prime. Today the Trust has a considerable investment in the fertile acres of South Lincolnshire around Spalding, being one of the largest landlords in an area where Halley and Richard Winfrey once campaigned so successfully for allotments and smallholdings for the labouring classes. Now, with that battle long forgotten, the Trust's holdings demonstrate large-scale farm management and modern agricultural methods at their best in a day when efficient production is the country's first requirement. The Trust began acquiring farms in the Spalding area during the 1939-44 War, when investment problems were acute and when enemy bombing not only made property purchase risky but actually damaged some of the London buildings from which the Trust drew rents.[1]

Spalding Urban Council agreed that the four or more acres in the town purchased by the Trust should be used in perpetuity for recreation under the name 'The Sir Halley Stewart Playing Field'. This official title takes us back to 1932, when Halley consented to figure among the knights bachelor in the New Year Honours List. It was well known that he could have

[1] The estate manager currently looking after the Trust's farming interests is James Crowden, of Elworthy and Grounds, estate agents. He is a grandson of Dr Crowden of Gedney Hill, named in chapter five as being associated with Richard Winfrey in acquiring the *Spalding Guardian* in 1887.

been honoured in greater ways at an earlier stage but had consistently declined, conviction turning him against hereditary titles. The knighthood was, in fact, offered almost by return of post after he had declined a baronetcy. How could one act otherwise who had spent so much of his strength in fighting under the banner of Gladstone and Asquith against the power of the House of Lords? In 1888 Halley had copied out some sarcastic verses on the subject which were still among his papers at death. Should sons, no matter how criminal, stupid, ignorant or defective, succeed their fathers as pilots, surgeons, parsons and judges simply on the ground of sonship?, the verses asked.

> What mattered lack of knowledge or the evil
>   they had done,
> While each claimed his proud position as his
>   father's eldest son?
> God preserve the fine old fetish, full of
>   sweetness and of light,
> That big bulwark of our freedom, called
>   'Hereditary Right'!
> Which, to driveller and drunkard, and the
>   dastard virtue shuns,
> Means the right to govern Britain in the House
>   of eldest sons.

But by 1932, in the serenity of his ninety-fourth year, the honour came not only for earlier political activity but for benefactions and for social and public services. He failed by only a few months to be the oldest man ever to receive the accolade—and, in fact, sought unsuccessfully to postpone the honour for the short time needed to attain this unique distinction!

However, he was the only one of those at the ceremony on February 25th to whom King George V had anything to say. The possibility of this had crossed Halley's mind and while waiting to kneel before the King, he asked one of the equerries what he should do if the King spoke to him. 'Don't worry,' was the reply, 'His Majesty never does.' 'That's not an answer to my question' was Halley's immediate rejoinder. National figures honoured on the same day included a fellow Congregationalist, Sir Harold Bellman, Abbey Road Building Society; Sir Henry Dale, National Institute for Medical Research, Hampstead; Sir John Hammerton, editor, Universal Encyclopaedia; Sir Henry Wellcome, Wellcome Foundation and associated research centres; and Sir Henry Wilkins, president, Co-operative Wholesale Society Ltd. For this Palace ceremony Halley felt that a man of his years need not replace his morning coat, despite its great age, and he would not have worn a new coat but for the fact that one of his sons insisted on taking him to be measured for one, and paid for it!

Halley meanwhile celebrated his ninety-fourth birthday on January 18th by lunching with his son Percy at his home, 128 Park Lane, where Ramsey Macdonald, then Prime Minister, was a guest. Celebrations followed at The Red House, where he entertained his children and grandchildren. At the wish of the trustees, Halley in October 1933 signed a deed altering the name of the Trust from the 'Halley Stewart Trust Fund' to the 'Sir Halley Stewart Trust'.

A coat of arms had already been granted to Halley as far back as February 1922. The College of Arms interpret these armorial bearings in everyday terms as follows: The lower part of the shield consists of silver and blue checks; the upper part is gold. On the upper part is a broad black vertical band charged with a gold portcullis. Against the remaining gold are two black ancient galleys with sails furled. The Crest has a Lymphad (galley) as in the shield between two gold fleurs-de-lis. The crest stands on a crest wreath of twisted silk in blue and gold, with the mantling—in Halley's livery colours of blue lined with gold—falling away on either side of the helm, which is such as is appropriate to a gentleman without title.[1]

Halley no doubt intended the fleur-de-lis, representing the crown of Lorraine, to recall his father's imprisonment in the Fortress of Biche in that part of France. The alternate silver and blue checks are frequently found in the arms of families named Stewart, and the portcullis without chains is not only the badge of Westminster but may also be a further reference to the fortress of Biche. The galley, which is the crest and also in chief on the shield, offers other associations, for it represents the Lymphad of Lorne. The Marquess of Lorne is the eldest son of the Duke of Argyle, Head of the Campbells, but this was originally a very early Stewart title and was taken from them with their lands by the Campbells. The galley is also a reminder of the ship in which Alexander Stewart ran away to sea, and may also recall Halley's maritime associations through his residence in coastal Sussex and his Parliamentary election at Greenock.

But of deeper family significance is the motto, 'There remaineth a rest,' for this text from the Bible (Hebrews chapter IV, 9) was Alexander Stewart's own

---

[1] Arms: Per Fess Or and Chequery Argent and Azure in chief on a Pale of the third between two Lymphads sails furled Sable a Portcullis of the first. Crest: A Lymphad as in the Arms between two Fleurs-de-Lis Or.

motto, engraved on his personal seal which also bore an impression of a three-masted sailing ship. Alexander's children looked upon this motto and text as their family crest. The seal passed as an heirloom to Ebenezer, who also valued and always wore on his watch chain a gold locket—a wedding gift to him from his bride—on which the ship and motto were engraved on the back, with his initials on the front.[1]

Rest for Halley, however, was something which still lay ahead. He declined, he told a local reporter about this time, to curl up and wait the inevitable end, and stories of his vitality abound. A *Herts Advertiser* report recalls him being chided for running to catch a train at the age of eighty-eight. 'At the worst,' he explained, 'it means only sudden death and what better end could a man wish for?' John Derry—who had helped Halley's Spalding campaign, joined Winfrey's newspaper team, took editorships at Nottingham and Sheffield, and retired to Bournemouth—had a day trip to Harpenden in December 1926 which both he and Halley described in letters to Richard Winfrey. 'I had him end on for four-and-a-quarter hours and either his tongue or mine was going the whole time,' wrote Halley. 'We were not afraid to launch out into the deep, away from the shallows and narrows. But back to shore again, of

[1] Both seal and locket passed into Mr Guthrie Stewart's possession. George Stewart's poem, composed to mark the golden wedding of Alexander and Ann in 1874, included these lines:
    For O, how true while yet we're here
      That graving on his seal!
    And O, how certainly that truth
      We altogether feel,
    That life, however rough or smooth,
      A voyage must be confessed!
    And O, how sweet it is to know
      'For us remains a rest!'

course, with our spoils from the great deep. . . .'
Derry recalled: 'He was on the platform. He had walked there, and we walked back to his house, largely uphill, for a long half-mile. His intellectual alertness never seemed one whit abated or flagging. He was affectionately confiding. He told me much about his business success and all about his Trust. He said he is worth half-a-million and his son Percy much more. . . . Finally he persisted in walking back with me to the station and seeing me off.'

On Halley's ninetieth birthday (January 18, 1928) he made a great impression on R. E. Lovegrove, Harpenden representative of the *Luton News*, who said the interview with him was quite the most memorable of his career. In sprightly fashion, the old man stepped into the billiards room where he was waiting, a buttonhole from the garden brightening his dark suit. He talked animatedly of his father's imprisonment, his two business fortunes, and the international situation, before reciting a passage from Shakespeare. Then he demonstrated some shots on the billiards table, saying that one of his most skilful opponents was Leslie Burgin, a Harpenden resident who became MP for Luton and a Minister of the Crown. It was the ever-vigilant Finding who finally suggested the interview should end. Two days later Halley made his way to Castor House, near Peterborough, to join his old friend Sir Richard Winfrey in another visit to the Lincolnshire Small Holdings Association, of which they had been president and chairman respectively for well over thirty years. In Spalding, Halley entertained the tenants to luncheon as part of his birthday celebrations. He was there that day, he told them, not as their guest but as their host, to pay them honour and homage and to mark the progress made since he first appealed in Spalding for the emancipation of the agricultural labourer. Percy Malcolm supported his father at the function and announced his wish to mark Halley's birthday by purchasing a farm to add to the Association's holdings.

Another birthday gesture by Percy was a contribution of £90 to the fund organized by Halley to help Nonconformist ministers in times of financial distress. Percy's warm-hearted support of his father's schemes was, in fact, a joy to the old man. One of its most notable expressions was Percy's gift of £10,000 to the fund to extend the Mansfield House Settlement in Canning Town, where social work among Eastenders was carried out under the auspices of Mansfield College, Oxford, the Congregational theological college. The Duke of York (later George VI), opening the extension in March 1931, mentioned this gift as a son's tribute to Halley, who for many years was treasurer and chairman of the Settlement. Declining Percy's invitation to meet the Duke and Duchess at this function, Halley wrote: 'It was your show. And when I read what the Duke so kindly said about me I bless my stars that I was not there to hear it.' Among many other gestures by which Percy sought to show his respect for his father was his commission to the sculptor Doyle Jones to execute a bust of Halley in 1926. This is now in the possession of the London Brick Company and has a place of honour at the brick works.

In 1927 Percy had turned down an invitation to become prospective Liberal candidate for Boston. Though Halley would have been pleased to see the family connection with Lincolnshire Liberalism continued, Percy's divergent views on Free Trade might well have proved an embarrassment. However, in 1929 Halley himself was honoured by election as president of the Spalding Liberal Association and had the excitement very soon after of seeing a Liberal again returned to Parliament in the person of James Blindell. Telegraphing the result of the by-election, Blindell exultantly told Halley: 'Your historic victory for Liberalism repeated today in your old Division.' Harpenden Liberals similarly claimed Halley as president. With typical fighting spirit he had formed the Association in 1924, the year that a Liberal garden party at Kings Langley was attended by Mr and Mrs Lloyd George and by Mrs Asquith. It was the first appearance of the two families together in public since the reunion of the Liberals a year earlier. Speaking there, Mrs Asquith—the celebrated Margot—was glad to see 'that stalwart of Liberalism, Mr Halley Stewart, among us. Liberalism in Harpenden *is* Mr Stewart. To him it is more than a party, it is a religion' . . .

Production of bricks at the Wootton Pillinge works was nearing 120 million per year when Percy succeeded his father as chairman of the London Brick Company. Output in 1910 had been 48 million, and by 1936 it was running at 120 million, with 500 people employed at the works, making it the largest single brick-producing plant in the world. By then the dreams of Halley and Percy of workers' homes in a garden village setting and of enlightened employment conditions had been realized. The character of the original hamlet had been entirely changed and as its name was a little unwieldy for the fast-growing works, a new title was sought. By a happy inspiration, the family name of the former and present chairman, Halley and Percy, was taken and the village became known as Stewartby. In due course the inhabitants requested local government powers for themselves and the first meeting of Stewartby parish council was held on October 1, 1937. Percy had reported to the shareholders in March 1931 that wages paid were 120 per cent higher than pre-war, the working week was down to 48 hours from 56, the week's holiday was granted with pay, and the year had seen the fifth distribution of cash bonus under the profit-sharing scheme. The *Investors' Review* in January 1931 wrote of the London Brick Company that from the outset it had applied itself to reducing the import of foreign bricks from countries where labour conditions compared unfavourably with our own. Productive capacity had been increased, prices lowered, labour conditions improved by rationalization, and profits ploughed back. The company's growth and activity showed a high degree of organization and vision.

Percy's conduct of the business was, in fact, outstandingly successful, and he went on to surpass his father as a man of substance. The homes built at Stewartby for old servants of the London Brick Company from designs by Professor Sir Albert Richardson, president of the Royal Academy, were among the fruits of his own charitable trust set up in 1945. Percy died in 1951 and the homes were opened in 1956 by Beatrice Lady Stewart, his widow. He had inherited something of his mother's winning disposition as well as Halley's acumen, and had a charm which endeared him to worker and director alike and made it easy for him to carry a company board room with him. He was able to put into effect in the London Brick Company the enlightened schemes which occurred to him and to Halley, and on the basis of these experiments encouraged their adoption in the cement-making enterprises also.

On a summer Sunday afternoon in 1930, Halley was at Stewartby to open the new village hall, incorporating a memorial to Stewartby men who fell in the Great War. Its pillared portico looks across the village green towards the main offices, to which Percy regularly travelled from his home at The Lodge, Sandy (now headquarters of the Royal Society for the Protection of Birds); and the names of eighty men appear on four stone panels in the memorial vestibule. Another milestone in Stewartby history—in which Halley insisted in sharing despite fears for his health—was the visit of Prince George, Duke of Kent, to the village and brickworks in October 1935, when the Royal visitor started a fountain playing to mark the occasion.

In the last few years of his life, as Halley's excursions became fewer and briefer, The Red House and Harpenden itself increasingly gave him an outlet. One room in the house was being used as a free library for the town, having been opened in October 1925 by Sir Richard Lodge, Professor of History at Edinburgh University and brother of Sir Oliver Lodge, a resident of Harpenden. The latter was one of the local people with whom Halley was glad to discuss affairs. Among others were Mr E. Cassleton Elliott, accountant and fellow Congregationalist, who also advised on financial management; Mr Sutherland Graeme, barrister and chairman of the governors of the Memorial Nursing Centre; Mr Percy Raby Mare, business man; and Mr Harry Otto Thomas, newspaper director. These four were the first trustees of the Harpenden Scholars Fund, with Mr Peter Wood (solicitor) secretary.

An unusual personal interest for Halley in 1930 was to sit for his portrait, a young artist attending at The Red House for this. John Frye Bourne was only eighteen and a third-year student at the Royal Academy Schools when his father was invited to become minister of Harpenden Congregational Church. His mother stayed at The Red House for a few nights so that she could get the manse in order before the family moved in, and Halley persuaded Louise (Mrs Haram) to come down to be company for her. The two became good friends, and thereafter both Mr and Mrs Bourne paid many visits to the house.

Halley was, of course, an honoured member of the Congregational Church at Harpenden. Ministers valued his support and fellowship, and The Red House and garden were often used for church events. When Mrs Bourne, as wife of the minister, once requested the use of the gardens Halley asked: 'And what do you expect me to do?' 'You can give a plain tea,' she confidently replied. 'And what is a plain tea?' 'A plain tea means tea, milk, sugar, bread and butter and scones.' 'No cakes?' queried the host. 'No. The ladies will provide home-made cakes themselves.' Having thus clearly defined the responsibility, Halley accepted it, and the bakehouse provided loaves, scones and drop scones at his order. The latter were unfortunately described on the baker's bill as 'Scotch pancakes' and on paying it Halley struck out this item and sent a cheque for the rest. 'No cakes. That was the agreement,' exclaimed Halley when the minister mentioned the matter, and as Halley—with disconcerting exactness—invariably said what he meant and meant what he said, the minister himself had to pay the balance!

Asked by Mrs Bourne if he would sit for her son, Halley—after confirming that he would not be asked or expected to buy the picture—agreed as a gesture of help to the youth. As John felt he could not expect sittings of sixty or ninety minutes from a man aged ninety-two, he arranged to have ten sittings of thirty minutes each, planning to make drawings and notes and to work from these and from memory on the canvas in his studio at home.

So age and youth faced each other regularly in Halley's book-lined room, the plan working perfectly except that they always had a friendly difference of opinion as to the time given to it. Miss Finding showed John into the room and at the end Halley always went out with him to the front steps to say Goodbye. John punctiliously checked his watch when he started to draw and ended the sitting inside the agreed thirty minutes. Halley, however, measured the minutes from Finding's announcement to the parting on the steps, even if time had been taken in chatting after the sitting. So his farewell would often be like this: 'Goodbye . . . Thirty-four-and-a-half minutes this morning!'

John, conscious of the honour of being indulged by such a person as Halley, was jubilant to find how excited he was to see the finished canvas. Halley asked to keep it a few days, and Finding saw he had set it up at the foot of his bed. It was evident that he wanted to have it, and equally evident that he was reluctant to go back on his first decision against buying it. Louise stepped in by paying John £25 for his work and after framing she took it away. The youthful painter had made the most of his opportunity. Apart from producing an excellent likeness, much treasured in her home today by Louise's daughter, Dr Joan

Haram, he included in the background several items characteristic of the room. A corner of the safe showed behind Halley's shoulder, with legal papers and red tape lying on it. A chessboard leaned beside it. Above it were books, and part of a glass-fronted bookcase. After World War II John was persuaded by Louise (against his will) to alter the background—possibly to conform in style with other paintings in the house—so that these intriguing details are not now to be found in this interesting (and for the artist, very promising) work.

It was Mr Bourne who started a monthly sheet of church news and headed it: 'Harpenden Congregational Church (Minister—The Rev A. A. Bourne)'. When Halley saw it he at once telephoned to point out an error. Quoting the heading, he assured the minister it was inaccurate. 'You are *not* a parenthesis,' he told him.

15. THE HUNDREDTH YEAR

MUCH care and time were given to negotiating arrangements for The Red House to go to the town on Halley's death, to afford an extension to the work of the Memorial Nursing Centre and to give opportunity for establishing Harpenden's first cottage hospital. Mr Otto Thomas, presiding over the public gathering which agreed to accept Halley's offer, said there had never been a more interesting meeting in Harpenden. Halley felt that the estate, comprising the house with nearly seven acres, three cottages and other buildings, in a quiet central road, was admirably adaptable. In view of current hospital policy, he worded the deed of gift in 1929 so that use as a hospital was left open but the activities of the Nursing Centre were completely safeguarded. Towards the cost of adaptation, Halley arranged for a donation of £1,000, provided Harpenden raised £3,000 within four years of taking over the property. In the summer of 1932 he held a fete in the grounds to raise funds for the Nursing Centre and this was an opportunity for residents to inspect the house.[1]

Halley's much-quoted remark that he did not want to die disgracefully rich was reported at the time of Harpenden's public consideration of the gift of The Red House. Within two weeks he received two thousand begging letters with requests for assistance. One asked for a car; another wanted a loan of £5,000.

[1] A tablet in the house recalls that it was, in fact, opened two years after Halley's death as a hospital for general and maternity cases, with health clinics and nursing centre. When a patients' sitting-room was presented by the League of Friends of the hospital, the Trust gave furniture and equipment in memory of Dr Bernard Stewart.

He was glad that only one of the letters came from Harpenden, and commented: 'If I had money to give away like they think I have, I could have got rid of it before I reached my ninety-second year.'

Naturally many requests were made to Halley, and dealing with them kept his pen much occupied, for always he preferred in reply to be explanatory rather than perfunctory. One lady wrote to say she was collecting for a wheel chair for a deserving woman, and had in fact already purchased the chair so that its use could be enjoyed without further delay. She was sure Halley would like to help, and quoted the price paid. Characteristic of him, though no doubt a surprise to the lady, came a reply which ran like this: 'As the lady already has the wheel chair and as it is already paid for, I cannot see how this poor lady can in any way be helped by any contribution from me.'

A condition of the gift of the estate to the town was that the donor should be allowed to continue to live there rent free, and he delighted thereafter to describe himself as the tenant. He remained so for perhaps much longer than he or anyone else expected, despite well-known Stewart longevity. It was this family characteristic which moved him in August 1932 to write a letter to *The Times* in which he noted with evident satisfaction: 'My parents, my father being eighty-four years of age, kept their golden wedding in 1874, one brother his in 1904, and another his in 1915 when I was seventy-seven.'

Certain local organizations were able to meet at The Red House. In 1932, reminiscing to the Toc H branch, Halley claimed that at fourteen he could recite Matthew 25 in Greek. In 1935, the League of Nations Union branch met there under his chairmanship and re-elected him president despite his objections. 'I am constantly being asked to take up new work and I am constantly declining it,' he had to explain. 'I don't get up so early now and I go to bed three or four hours earlier. My work in the past used to last until 3 a.m. but I have given that up now.'

Halley had no illusions about his health and, though he took reasonable care of himself and could rely on the healthful effect of a life of sustained self-discipline, must often have wondered at the way he was spared. In 1933, he had had another of his serious illnesses and was assured that recovery was impossible. 'My three doctors agreed that mine was a hopeless case, and now say that they had never previously seen or heard of such a recovery as mine at $95\frac{1}{2}$ years. You will find me a little slow,' he wrote to Stanley Unwin in July, 'but I have been clear-headed all through the last eleven weeks. My ailment is simply physical weakness.' Laid aside, he had even more time to think—of the joys and blessings of life, the rewards of service, the consolations of faith, the pursuit of truth, the ills of the world and the burdens of its people. He could write with exquisite tenderness when he felt a message of sympathy was needed.

Halley could also pull the legs of his friends with delicate irony. One of them was Gerrard Nonus Ford, a Congregationalist who in retirement moved to North Wales and on reaching his eightieth birthday, was pleased to share his joy at doing so by writing to many old friends. He told Halley he had marked the birthday by resigning from eleven London committees. Halley at once replied: 'Dear Gerrard. If you had taken my advice and come to live near London instead of burying yourself in North Wales, you would not have had to give up all this good work when you are still a comparatively young man.'

Halley used a golden key when asked, in 1932, to open the new church at Hatfield, of which he had laid the foundation stone. It was the first to be financed by the Hertfordshire Congregational extension fund and so represented the first fruits of the harvest for which Halley had planned and waited. He had preached in every Congregational church in the county, and his ardent advocacy of extension showed how strong was his faith in the continuing role of the denomination and in its message. Another addition which particularly appealed to him in 1935 was the new church on the Heddon Court estate at Cockfosters, for his father had conducted services in cottages at Cockfosters a hundred years before.

Harpenden is a pleasant town. Halley went to it when it was still a village, and was glad to play a part in preserving its open approach from the St Albans direction by underwriting the cost of the manorial rights of the Common when bought by the council. He gave £2,500 to cover the land, and the council paid £500 for two cottages on the Common. This was in 1935, silver jubilee year of King George V and a time for general rejoicing. Halley shared in it, joining 300 residents whose ages exceeded sixty-five in a jubilee supper at Harpenden. Oldest one among them, he gave each of the other guests a quarter-pound of tea as a jubilee present.

There had been a special visit to London in April 1935 when Halley motored to the Hyde Park Hotel to attend a dinner given in Percy's honour by the National Industrial Alliance. This was in tribute to Malcolm's energetic service as Commissioner for Special Areas, a thankless responsibility accepted in 1934 at the request of the Conservative Government to help the unemployed in South Wales and Durham.

Halley was proud of this development, saying his ambition was that his family should render service of the kind his son was seeking to give. Malcolm was a fearless critic and never hesitated to expose conditions in the special areas, and it must have been a great blow to him and to Halley later when in 1936 Malcolm felt he had to resign the office because of difficulties with the Treasury.

Jubilee year saw Halley again re-elected president of the local branch of the League of Nations Union, and in the General Election of the same year, as president of the Liberal Association, he took the chair on the Liberal platform. But this time there was no spell-binding address. He who, but for a slight huskiness of speech, might have been one of the greatest orators of his generation, had now to explain that after eighty years of platform work, and activity in every General Election since 1852, he had completed his share of public speaking. However, in November he officially opened the Austral, a new cinema in Harpenden, his interest in this being that proceeds from the first performance were destined for the Nursing Centre.

A family event of note which marked the year 1935 must also have been the last religious service which Halley conducted, when he baptized his great grandson, Bernard Harold Ian Halley Stewart. The baby's father was Professor Harold C. Stewart (London University and St Mary's Hospital Medical School, Paddington), the elder of Bernard's sons and with his brother, Mr Gerald Halley Stewart of the British Ceramic Society, among today's trustees.[1]

---

[1] The personal link between the Trust and the medical world which was provided by Bernard and continues through Professor Stewart was strengthened in 1965 by the appointment as a trustee of

A salute to Sir Halley, written by Dr Albert Peel, appeared in *The Christian World* in January 1936 just before he celebrated his ninety-eighth birthday. 'During his long life in business, in politics and in religion, no party machine or centralized authority has ever had Halley Stewart in its pocket,' he wrote. Two days after the birthday, the country mourned the death of George V. The Prince of Wales (later the Duke of Windsor) came to the throne. Thereafter the year 1936 moved quietly onwards for Halley. He did not go far or frequently from The Red House, but made no secret of his final ambition—to live to be a hundred years old. This would be distinction indeed to form a topstone to the rest. With Miss Finding at hand to keep him from the risks inevitable when a man's brimming interests far outrun his physical resources, Halley seemed likely to achieve it.

It was during 1936 that Halley at last gave up attending meetings of the London Brick Company board. Miss Finding always went with him to the offices and saw him safely home again, waiting near the board room while he was engaged. Arthur Warboys clearly remembered his last visit on May 26th to Africa House, LBC headquarters in Kingsway. 'He sat next to Percy. The meeting went on, but he took no part. After a time he looked at his watch and said "I must go". He never came to another meeting.'

At Stewartby, where the children had had to travel to other villages for education, a school had now been built by Bedfordshire County Council on a site and with bricks given by the company. Halley was planning to attend the opening ceremony, performed by Oliver Stanley, President of the Board of Education,

Halley's grand-daughter, Dr Joan Haram, pathologist at the Elizabeth Garrett Anderson Hospital.

in January 1937. Another tribute appeared in *The Christian World* to announce his ninety-ninth birthday —and the start of his hundredth year—on January 18th. 'Nonconformity,' it said, 'has no more distinguished layman than Sir Halley Stewart, and we welcome a suggestion made by Dr A. G. Sleep that his fellow Free Churchmen should gladden the day for him by brief personal messages of congratulation and good cheer.'

His old friend Sir Richard Winfrey had been among Halley's Christmastime visitors and in his paper, the *Peterborough Advertiser*, recorded that his conversation was as illuminating and as wise as ever. Percy, Bernard and Louise were among members of the family who joined their father for his birthday party. One of the things that made it especially joyful for Halley was that Percy had just been created a baronet in the New Year Honours, in overdue recognition of his place as industrial statesman and public servant, particularly in regard to the distressed areas.[1]

However, the good health of the old man that was noticeable at the family party was interrupted a day or so later by a mild influenza. Halley had throughout life suffered from bronchial attacks, sometimes severely so, but there was no thought of such an emergency when Miss Finding summoned the doctor as a precaution. But bronchitis had developed by the time Dr Bernard Stewart, who was then living in retirement at Totteridge, came over to see his father.

[1] Halley and Percy had given the family name to the Bedfordshire brickmaking village of Wootton Pillinge when it was re-named Stewartby, and Percy adopted this as part of the title in 1937 when he became Sir Malcolm Stewart of Stewartby. Although he had always been addressed as Percy, he preferred on creation to use his more Scottish second Christian name of Malcolm but retained the initial P., being usually known as Sir P. Malcolm Stewart.

And so, at ninety-nine, the valiant heart found itself struggling in its final conflict. This time the odds were soon seen to be hopeless, and death claimed all that was mortal of Halley Stewart at 11.25 on the night of January 26th.

'Our Grand Old Man has gone from us before he had attained the century on which his heart was set, for with his usual keenness he had entered the unequal contest with Time. Well, Time has won,' said Dr Sidney Berry in his funeral address, 'but it is a victory which inflicts no hurt upon the loser, and if he were here, he would jest about it. We are the losers. . . .' In the church at Harpenden where Halley had faithfully worshipped, surrounded by so many from religious, political and social service organizations who came to remember and to grieve, Dr Berry sought in that simple service to pay tribute to the giant they mourned.

'He was a great personality, strong, distinctive, challenging, but never just assertive as with smaller men. He loved voices but hated echoes. He believed with his whole heart that a man's true worth to God and to the world lay in his expression of his real belief, never in tame conformity with conventional standards. He held that God gave man as His Divinest gift a mind with which to think things out, and in fellowship with others and in the clash of opinions to come nearer to the final truth of things.'

With a grace and understanding that made the moments moving and memorable, Dr Berry touched on Halley's tremendous sense of God, his reverence for truth, his service to men, his charity which never pauperized, his Spartan self-discipline, and his rejection of luxury and self-indulgence. 'In an age of echoes and conformities, he stands out rugged and distinct with his strong individuality. In an age which has so largely deserted religion, his life carried with it a message of the triumph of faith. In an age where so many have never moved beyond selfishness, his life sounds the clear note of service. Our prayer is that men of his strong fibre may never be lacking in this world.'

After cremation at Hendon, burial took place in Christ Church cemetery, St Albans Road, Barnet—'with all simplicity', as Halley had desired in his will. 'And I wish that between the time of death and the interment of the ashes, no blinds may be drawn to exclude God's cheer from the house of mourning.'

In Barnet he had seen all that was left of Jane laid to rest twelve lonely years before. Here, too, were the graves of some of their children. Barnet was his birthplace. Here he had saved his first pennies. Here he had first glimpsed those visions in pursuit of which he had grown great. Barnet was his home. Now he was back there—at home at last.

Percy Malcolm, Bernard and Louise were executors of their father's will and, in accordance with his wishes, shared between them personal effects from The Red House as mementoes. Halley left his children no money, declaring them to be already rich in gifts, inheritance, work and thrift; and bequeathed the whole of the residue of the estate, some £109,000 net, to the Trust 'to serve the one family of which we are all members'.

APPENDICES

Lectures delivered under the auspices of the
SIR HALLEY STEWART TRUST

1926 Science and Human Progress   Sir Oliver Lodge

1927 Christ and Society   Bishop Gore

1928 The Ordeal of this
      Generation   Gilbert Murray

1929 Equality   R. H. Tawney

1930 Health and Social
      Evolution   Sir George Newman

1931 The World's Economic
      Crisis   Sir Arthur Salter
            Sir Josiah Stamp
            J. M. Keynes
            Sir Basil Blackett
            Sir W. H. Beveridge
            Henry Clay

1932 From Chaos to Control   Sir Norman Angel

1933 The Way to Social Peace   Wickham Steed

1934 Is War Obsolete?   Canon C. E. Raven

1935 Scientific Progress   Sir James Jeans
            Sir William Bragg
            Professor E. V. Appleton
            Professor E. Mellanby
            Professor J. B. S. Haldane
            Professor Julian Huxley

1936 Aspects of a Changing
      Social Structure   Sir Percy Alden

1937 The World's Economic
      Future   A. Loveday
            J. B. Condliffe
            B. Ohlin
            E. F. Heckscher
            S. de Madariaga

1938 Rich Man, Poor Man   John Hilton

1948 The Atomic Age   Professor M. L. Oliphant
                                   Professor P. M. S. Blackett
                                   R. F. Harrod
                                   Lord Russell
                                   Lionel Curtis
     (Lecture not delivered but
        printed)   Professor D. W. Brogan

1961 Some Problems of the
     Pharmaco-Kinetics of
     Anaesthetics   Dr R. A. Butler, M.B.,
                                   Ch.B., Sir Halley Stewart
                                   Research Fellow

THE SIR HALLEY STEWART TRUST
List of Trustees from the foundation of the Trust in 1924

	Date of appointment	Death (or resignation)
Sir Halley Stewart	Dec. 15, 1924	Jan. 26, 1937
Mr Reginald Halley Stewart	Dec. 15, 1924	April 22, 1926
Sir P. Malcolm Stewart Bt.	Dec. 15, 1924	Feb. 27, 1951
Dr Bernard Halley Stewart	Dec. 15, 1924	July 30, 1958
Rev. Dr Sidney Malcolm Berry	Dec. 15, 1924	Aug. 1961
Rev. Dr Thomas Hywell Hughes	Dec. 15, 1924	Aug. 1945
Rev. Dr Albert Peel	Dec. 15, 1924	Nov. 1949
Mr Harold Beaumont Shepheard	Dec. 15, 1924	R Dec. 1950 D Dec. 1965
Sir Stanley Unwin, KCMG	Jan. 22, 1926	*
Sir Percy Alden	Oct. 2, 1928	June 30, 1944
Mr Richard Pattinson Winfrey	July 4, 1946	*
Major J. McL. Short	Dec. 13, 1950	R Nov. 1965
Professor Harold Charles Stewart	Dec. 13, 1950	*
Sir Ronald Compton Stewart, Bt.	Mar. 25, 1952	*
Mr Gerald Halley Stewart	June 16, 1959	*
Dr B. Joan Haram	Nov. 10, 1965	*

* Trustees still serving, 1968.

FAMILY TREE I

	ELIZABETH b. Nov. 25, 1824 d. May 12, 1897	m. Jul. 25, 1860	Michael Quin b. Feb. 29, 1790 d. Dec. 5, 1870
	ALEXANDER b. May 26, 1826 d. Ap. 1, 1885	m. (1) Mar. 15, 1856	Sarah Dilworth b. Dec. 31, ? d. Dec. 15, 1874
		m. (2) Nov. 1, 1876	Francis Caroline Southwell b. Nov. 1, 1845 d. ? 1915
	PHILIP b. Dec. 6, 1827 d. Dec. 13, 1908	m. Dec. 21, 1854	Margaret Montague Murray b. May 15, 1830 d. Jun. 12, 1908
	GEORGE b. Jul. 24, 1829 d. Jul. 27, 1923	m. Dec. 23, 1856	Adelaide Keen b. Ap. 29, 1832 d. Jan. 2, 1910
ALEXANDER STEWART	ANN b. Dec. 30, 1830 d. Nov. 24, 1831		
b. May 27, 1790 d. Nov. 3, 1874	KEZIA b. Ap. 11, 1832 d. May 1912	m. Ap. 9, 1870	Henry Hobson b. Mar. 10, 1823 d. Jul. 29, 1897
m. Jan. 13, 1824 —	ISABELLA b. Jul. 3, 1833 d. Dec. 8, 1853		
ANN KEZIA WHITE b. May 2, 1799 d. Ap. 5, 1875	EBENEZER b. Dec. 4, 1834 d. Jan. 24, 1914	m. Jan. 27, 1875	Mary Anne Betts b. May 3, 1844 d. Jul. 16, 1927
	MARTHA b. May 13, 1836 d. Aug. 1875	m. Jul. 20, 1866	Richard Knowles Spencer b. Jun. 27, 1843 d. Mar.(?) 1929
	HALLEY b. Jan. 18, 1838 d. Jan. 26, 1937	m. Jun. 20, 1865	Jane Elizabeth Atkinson b. Nov. 15, 1834 d. Dec. 26, 1924 *See Tree II*
	JOHN b. Jun. 24, 1839 d. Dec. 1, 1908	m. Jun. 27, 1864	Elizabeth Mary Porter b. Dec. 1, 1841 d. ?
	CHRISTIANA b. Jul. 30, 1841 d. Nov. 21, 1856		
	JOSIAH b. Aug. 11, 1843 d. Nov. 22, 1930	m. Mar. 22, 1881	Fanny Hinks b. Mar. 22, 1851 d. Aug. ? 1928
	JOSEPH b. Jan. 26, 1845 d. Ap. 29, 1938	m. (1) Mar. 8, 1875	Harriet Whitehouse b. Nov. 28, 1852 d. Dec. 8, 1905
		m. (2) Oct. 22, 1908	Violet Collins b. Jun. 4, 1884 marriage dissolved

FAMILY TREE II

HALLEY STEWART
b. Jan. 18, 1838
d. Jan. 26, 1937

m. Jun. 20, 1865 —

JANE ELIZABETH
ATKINSON

b. Nov. 15, 1834
d. Dec. 26, 1924

ERNEST HALLEY
b. Jul. 19, 1866
d. Jan. 26, 1867

HERBERT FOWLER
b. Jul. 12, 1867
d. Jan. 7, 1871

EDGAR HALLEY
b. Oct. 15, 1868
d. Oct. 31, 1868

REGINALD HALLEY m. Jun. 1, 1893   Kate Mildred
b. Oct. 15, 1868   Stevens
d. Ap. 22, 1926   b. Oct. 20, 1872
                                    d. Ap. 9, 1961
                                    See Tree III

BERTIE JANE   m. Oct. 11, 1902   Ernest Cecil
LOUISE   Haram
b. Jan. 8, 1871   b. Jul. 9, 1866
d. Mar. 28, 1961   d. Sept. 30, 1929
                                    See Tree IV

PERCY MALCOLM   m. (1) Jun. 30, 1896   Cordelia Rickett
b. May 9, 1872   b. Oct. 18, 1871
d. Feb. 27, 1951   d. Sept. 28, 1906

                 m. (2) Ap. 25, 1907   Beatrice Maud
                                        Pratt
                                        b. Aug. 15, 1879
                                        d. May 21, 1960
                                        See Tree V

EUSTACE HALLEY
b. May 6, 1874
d. Jun. 19, 1874

BERNARD HALLEY m. Ap. 11, 1905   Mabel Florence
b. May 6, 1874   Wyatt
d. Jul. 30, 1958   b. Dec. 27, 1884
                                    d.
                                    See Tree VI

FAMILY TREE III

REGINALD HALLEY STEWART m. Jun. 1, 1893 Kate Mildred Stevens
b. Oct. 15, 1868   b. Oct. 20, 1872
d. Ap. 22, 1926   d. Ap. 9, 1961

CHARLOTTE GLADYS   HERBERT GEORGE   DORIS MILDRED
HALLEY   HALLEY   HALLEY
b. Feb. 14, 1894   b. Aug. 4, 1897   b. Oct. 18, 1903
d.   d.   d.
 m. Jun. 18, 1919   m. (1) Jun. 21, 1917
   Oswald C. Pritchard   Dorothy Cove
   b.   b. 1896
   d.   d. Nov. 25, 1922

                             m. (2) Aug. 25, 1923
                                Caroline Finken
                                b.
                                d.

BRUCE GEORGE   ALFRED WILLIAM
b. Oct. 31, 1921   b. Ap. 13, 1923

FAMILY TREE IV

BERTIE JANE LOUISE STEWART m. Oct. 11, 1902   Ernest Cecil Haram
b. Jan. 8, 1871   b. Jul. 9, 1866
d. Mar. 28, 1961   d. Sept. 30, 1929

VIVIAN STEWART   BEATRICE JOAN
b. Nov. 21, 1903   b. Mar. 16, 1907
d.
   m. (1) Jun. 29, 1929
       Winifred Frances Baker
       b.
       d. Dec. 29, 1935
   m. (2) Oct. 18, 1938
       Sylvia Hester Brown
       b.
       d.

JOHN STEWART   JANE ELIZABETH
b. Ap. 9, 1946   b. Jun. 22, 1952

FAMILY TREE V

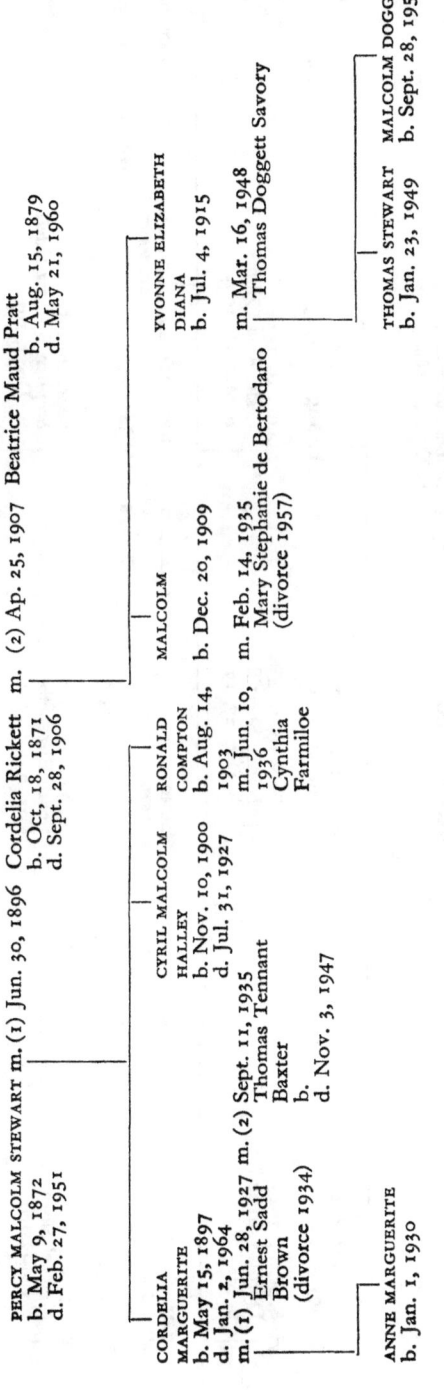

FAMILY TREE VI

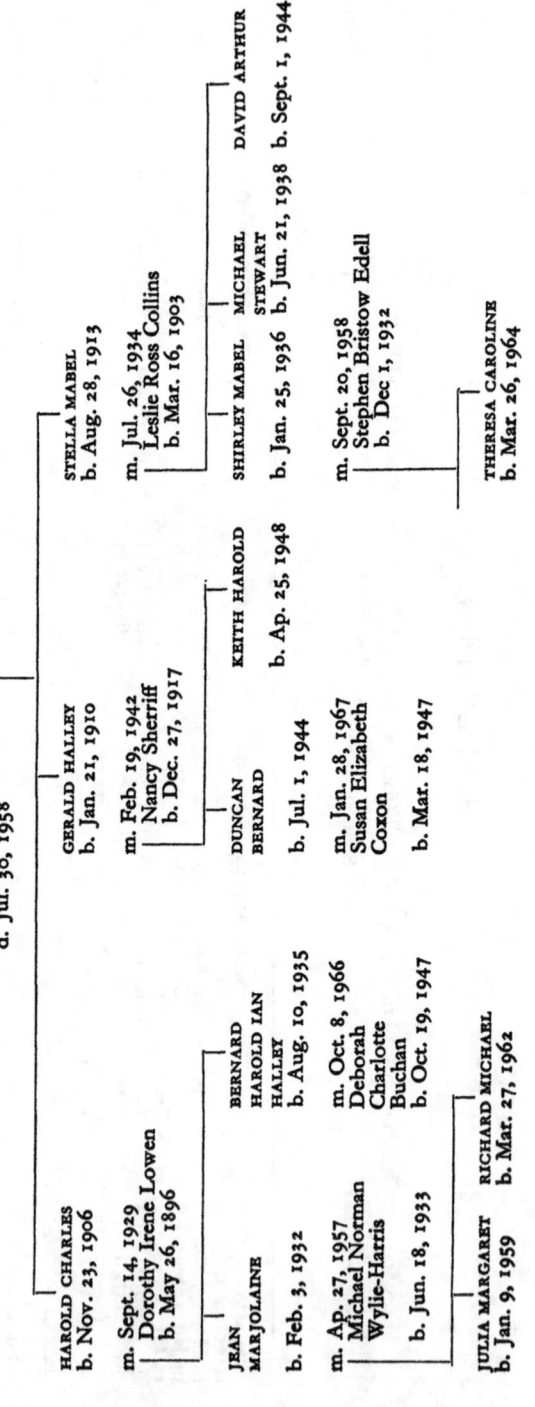

INDEX

(Abbr. HS—Sir Halley Stewart)

Allon, Henry, 33, 36, 41
Allotments, *see* Smallholdings
Appleton, Professor, 149
Arms, HS, coat of, 159–61
Asquith, H. H., 91, 100, 102
Asquith, Margot, 164
Associated Portland Cement Manufacturers Ltd., 106
Auger family, Burnham-on-Crouch, 124–5
Avis, H. A., 155

Barnet memories, 28–29; family graves, 178
Bartlett, J. R. (BOCM), 85–6
BBC programme on Alexander Stewart, 25
Beaufort House, Hastings, 40
Bellman, Sir Harold, 159
Berry, Dr Sidney, 119, 131, 152, 177
Bexhill, 41
Bible, attitude of HS to, 34, 131
Blindell, J., 164
BOCM, 85–8
Boer War, 90
Bonar Law, 91
Boston, Lincs., 46, 156, 163
Bourne, Rev. A. A., 167, 169
Bourne, John Frye (painter), 167–9
Branbridges, Kent, 38, 39, 44, 45
Brand, Hon. Arthur, 73
Bricks, 92, 105, 109, 111–12, 121, 164–5
Bulwick, Northants., 59, 62
Burgin, Leslie, M.P., 162
Burnham-on-Crouch, 124, 125

Campbell-Bannerman, Sir H., 90, 96, 97, 100
Cant, Elsie (Harpenden), 130; William, 118, 126–9
Carrington, Lord, 65, 78–9, 99
Cement, 92, 105–6
Chamberlain, Joseph, 48
Churchill, Winston, 91, 97
Clapham, Miss Barbara, 156
Clapham, 'The Firs', 76–7
Clark, Sir Andrew, 74
Clynes, J. R., 98

Coach traffic, 29
Collings, Jesse, 48, 53
Congregationalism, 38, 40–1, 76, 107, 111, 114, 118, 119, 146, 167, 173
County councils formed, 69
Croft Chapel, Hastings, 32–3, 40–1
Crowden, Dr J. T., 68, 157
Crowden, James, 157

Dale, Sir Henry, 159
Danish Bacon Company Ltd., 94
Derry, John, 161–2

East Midland Allied Press, 156
Education, HS withholds rate, 96; 1906 Bill, 99; Secular League, 114
Edward VII, 101, 102
Elliott, Cassleton, 166

Fergusson, Peter, 124
Finch-Hatton, Hon. Murray, 52, 54, 56, 58
Finding, Mary, 118, 129–30, 134, 175–6
Ford, Gerrard Nonus, 172
Forder, B. J. H., 92
Forder, B. J. & Co. Ltd., 92; *see also* Bricks

Gammon, Mary Goss, 118
George V, 102, 159, 173, 175
George VI, 163
George, Lloyd, 96, 97, 100, 102, 164
Gladstone, W. E., 32, 36, 63, 75, 90
Gold mines, 81
Graeme, Sutherland, 166
Greenock, 95–6, 97, 98, 101

Hammerton, Sir John, 159
Hampden, Viscount, 73
Hampstead Laboratory, 149
Haram, E. C., marries Louise, 94; *see also* Bertie Jane Louise Stewart
Haram, Dr Joan, 134, 138–9, 140, 175
Harcourt, Sir William, 66, 77
Hardie, Keir, M.P., 82, 98

Harpenden, cinema opening, 174; common rights, 173; Congregational Church, 115, 167, 169, 177; Nursing Centre and Hospital, 116, 170; Scholars Trust Fund, 150, 166; war memorial, 116
Harpenden, The Red House, 98, 126-7, 130, 134-5, 136, 167, 169, 170, 178
Hastings and St Leonard's, 32-5, 37, 40, 41, 42, 44, 72, 76, 155
Hastings and St Leonard's Times, 43-4, 45, 72
Hastings Observer, 43
Henderson, Arthur, 98
Herts. Advertiser, 161
Home Rule Bill, 56, 75
Howe, Alfred, 154
Hughes, Dr T. H., 119, 152, 156
Illustrated London News, 108
Ingram, Sir William, 46, 108
Insurance, National, 100
Ireland, HS visit, 70
Islington Chapel, 40, 43

Jane (HS wife), *see* Jane Elizabeth Stewart
Jones, Doyle (sculptor), 163

Keeble, George and Arthur (Peterborough), 92-3
Kent, Duke of, 166
Khaki Election, 91

Labour Party, 98, 113-14
Land values, 117
Lemon's school, 24, 27
Liberal Association, Spalding Women's Branch, 67; Eastern Counties Federation van, 70
Limehouse mill, 82
Lincolnshire Chronicle, 65
Lincolnshire Regiment, 110
Lodge, Sir Oliver, 140
Lodge, Sir Richard, 166
London Brick Company Ltd., 19, 121, 164, 175; *see also* Bricks
Lovegrove, R. E. (Harpenden journalist), 162
Lowell, James Russell, 138
Luton News, 162

Magistrates, HS views on; also HS appointment, 72-3
Mansfield, H. R. (Spalding candidate), 91

Mansfield House Settlement, 163
Mare, Percy Rabe, 166
Medical Research Council, 150-1
Monte Carlo casino (HS refused admission), 139
Morley, Lord, 101
MacDonald, Ramsey, 98, 159
McMillan, Miss Margaret (nursery), 143, 145

National Liberal Club, 44, 54, 72, 99
National Playing Fields Association, 142
Nicholls, George ('Sunrise' van), 70

O'Connor, John, M.P., 59; T.P., M.P., 59, 63
Oil cake mills, 38, 44-5, 48-50, 66, 80, 82, 83-9, 107
Oysters, 31; Auger family business, 124-5

Park Mansion, Hastings, 40, 62, 95, 155
Parliament, payment to Members, 71, 102
Parliament Bill, 102-3
Parnell divorce, 70-1
Peel, Dr Albert, 119, 145-6, 175
Pensions, old age, 100
Peterborough (HS a candidate), 90-1
Peterborough Advertiser, 82, 92
Pollock, Harry (Spalding candidate), 73-4, 77-8
Purvis, Sir Robert (Peterborough candidate), 91
Putterill, C. F. (Harpenden), 129

Ragged schools, 32, 35
Reid, James (Greenock candidate), 96-7
Research students, 150-3
Richardson, Sir Albert, 165
Rickett, Sir Compton, M.P., 80
Rochester, *see* Oil cake mills
Rochester & Chatham Journal, 48
Rosebery, Lord, 77
Rothamsted Agricultural Research Station, 150
Royal Society for the Protection of Birds (Sandy), 166

Scott Williamson, Dr M. C., 152
Sheffield Independent, 63
Shepheard, H. B., 119

Sleaford, 51
Smallholdings, 52, 64-5, 69, 78-9, 99, 110, 157, 162
Smith, Hugh Colin (BOCM), 86
Spalding (HS a candidate), 51-62, 73-4, 77-8
Spalding Liberals (trip to Park Mansion), 76
Spalding, Sir Halley Stewart Playing Field, 157
Spalding Guardian, 58, 67-8, 156
Spencer, Richard Knowles, 38, 86-7
Spurgeon's Orphanage, 77
Stamford, 51
Steed, Wickham, 141
Stevens, Vaughan, 126

* * *

STEWART FAMILY (noting relationship to HS):
Stewart, Alexander (father), 20-30, 36, 160
Stewart, Alexander (brother), 27
Stewart, Ann Kezia (mother), 25-7, 36-7
Stewart, Bernard Halley (son), 80, 94, 109, 111, 132-4, 140, 150, 156, 174, 176, 178
Stewart, Bernard Harold Ian Halley (great-grandson), 174
Stewart, Bertie Jane Louise (Mrs Haram, daughter), 94-5, 127, 134, 135, 140, 167, 168, 178
Stewart, Ebenezer (brother), 38, 39-40, 49, 83-8, 106, 154, 161
Stewart, Frank (nephew), 108
Stewart, George (brother), 31, 32, 37, 111, 161
Stewart, Gerald Halley (grandson), 174
Stewart, Grace (niece), 142, 154-5
Stewart, Guthrie (nephew), 107-9, 124, 161
STEWART, SIR HALLEY, Kt.:
Sir P. Malcolm Stewart's tribute, 19; character, 19-20; birth and background, 28-30; first jobs, 31-2; starts Hastings ministry, 33; independent in religion, 34, 42; in politics, 47, 63-4; marriage, 34; children, 36; protests at speeding carriages, 37; partnership with Ebenezer, 38, 45, 50, 154; Beaufort House and Park Mansion, 40; Islington pas-

STEWART, SIR HALLEY (*cont.*)
torate, 40, 43; leaves ministry, 42; Hastings newspaper, 43-4, 45, 72; Liberal agent and speaker, 43-4, 68; personal appearance, 37, 46, 63; oratory, 35, 66, 156, 174; sermon after mill fire, 49; Spalding candidate, 51-62, 73-4, 77-8; attitude to labour, 64, 65, 82, 98, 112, 113-14, 141, 165; Parliamentary attendance, 66; visits—United States, 66, Ireland, 70, Berlin, 100, Denmark, 99; views on Parnell, 71; appointed magistrate, 72; House of Lords, peerage, titles etc, 75, 99, 101, 102-3, 158; views on Labour Party, 98, 113-14; views on Gladstone, 32, 75; health, 68, 75, 96, 103-4, 172, 175; views on wealth and poverty, 55, 65-6, 71, 100; ragged schools, 32, 35; move to Clapham, 76-7; gold mines, 81; London mill project, 84-5; Rochester mill sold, 85-7; Peterborough candidate, 90-1; views on Boer War, 90; brick company formed, 92; resigns chair, 121; move to Luton, 92-3; financial management, 30, 31, 34, 50, 88, 95, 105-6, 117, 122-3, 135, 148; Greenock candidate, 95-7; provision company, 93; withholds education rate, 96; philanthropy, 116-20; repartee, 97, 109, 130, 133, 135, 136, 161, 169; buys The Red House, 98, 126-7; Royal diamond jubilee, 99; retires from Parliament, 100; listed as potential peer, 103; letter writer, 104, 137, 143-5; punctual, 105; mourns Philip, John, Kezia, Ebenezer, 106; golden wedding, 110, 136; private trust, 118; scholars trust, 150; biography in photographs, 122; wife's death, 125; carriages, horses, cars, 127-9; attitude to sons, 132-4; church attendance, 137, 167; versifier, 138-9; family prayers, 131, 136; food, 136; refused entrance to casino, 139; Fellow King's College, 149; knight bachelor and coat of arms, 157-61; runs to catch train, 161; worth half a million, 162; ninetieth birthday, 162-3;

STEWART, SIR HALLEY (*cont.*) comment by Royalty, 163; sculpture, 163; president Liberal Association, Spalding, 164, Harpenden, 164, 174; portrait, 167–9; begging letters, 170–1; recited in Greek, 171; last religious service, 174; aimed to be 100, 175; last Board meeting, 175; death, 177; will, 178; *see also* Trust

Stewart, Professor Harold Charles (grandson), 156, 174

Stewart, Jane Elizabeth (wife), school principal, 32, 34; appearance, 37; confidence in HS, 49; speaks at Spalding, 53; president women's Liberal branch, 67; family care, 81; Ebenezer's tribute, 88; The Red House memories, 104; death and an appreciation, 125–6; garden and driving out, 127–81, 137

Stewart, John (brother), 27, 41, 106, 107

Stewart, Josiah (brother), 39, 111, 118

Stewart, Kezia (sister), 32, 34, 106

Stewart, Martha (sister), 38, 39,

Stewart, Sir P. Malcolm (son), tribute to HS, 19; bonfire marks HS election, 74; election agent, 77; marriage, 80; supervises barges, 80; redeems men's suits, 82; chooses clock for HS, 88; bricks, 92, 105, 121, 124; cement, 105–6, 166; war work, 112; widowed, remarried, 132; host to Ramsey MacDonald, 159; HS ninetieth birthday, 163; declines candidature, 163; business approach, 165; home at Sandy, 166; death, 165; Commissioner for Special Areas, 173, 176; created baronet, 176; executor, 178

Stewart, Philip (brother), 27, 29, 31, 106, 107

Stewart, Reginald Halley (son), 36, 79, 93, 139, 154

Stewart, Sir Ronald Compton (grandson), 122, 124

* * *

Stewart Brothers and Spencer, *see* Oil cake mills
Stewart longevity, 171
Stewart Limited, provisions, 93, 142, 155
Stewartby, 165–6, 175
'Sunrise' van, 70

Thomas, Harry Otto, 166, 170
Trust, Sir Halley Stewart, formation and objects, 119–20; meetings and lectures, 139–41; chairmanship, 143; policy, 145, 147–8; Hampstead Laboratory, 149; reception for research students, 151–3; secretaryship, 154–6; investment in land, 157; new title, 159; family trustees, 119, 174; residue of estate, 178
Tryon, Admiral Sir George, 59–62, 69

Unilever, 85
Unwin, Sir Stanley, 142–3

Victoria, Queen, 20, 27, 30, 99
Victoria, H.M.S., 61

'Wardown', Luton, 92, 97
Wellcome, Sir Henry, 159
Wilkins, Sir Henry, 159
Winchilsea, Earl of, 52, 58
Windsor, Duke of, 175
Winfrey Avenue, Spalding, 157
Winfrey, Sir Richard, 52–8, 64, 67–9, 72, 73, 77–9, 81–2, 90–2, 95, 99, 103, 110, 156, 161–2, 176
Winfrey, Richard Francis, 52, 116
Winfrey, Richard Pattinson, 154–6
Wood, Peter (Harpenden), 166
Wootton Pillinge (Stewartby), 111, 124, 164, 176
Worboys, Sir Arthur, 123–4, 175
Wright, J. Macer (Hastings), 45, 72

For Product Safety Concerns and Information please contact our EU representative GPSR@taylorandfrancis.com
Taylor & Francis Verlag GmbH, Kaufingerstraße 24, 80331 München, Germany

www.ingramcontent.com/pod-product-compliance
Lightning Source LLC
Chambersburg PA
CBHW061447300426
44114CB00014B/1872